# Summary of Contents

# THE PRINCIPLES OF PROJECT MANAGEMENT

BY **MERI WILLIAMS**

# The Principles of Project Management

by Meri Williams

Copyright © 2008 SitePoint Pty. Ltd.

**Expert Reviewer**: Drew McLellan      **Editor**: Georgina Laidlaw
**Expert Reviewer**: Kevin Lawver      **Index Editor**: Fred Brown
**Managing Editor**: Simon Mackie      **Cover Design**: Alex Walker
**Technical Editor**: Toby Somerville
**Technical Director**: Kevin Yank
**Printing History**:
   First Edition: March 2008

## Notice of Rights

## Notice of Liability

## Trademark Notice

Published by SitePoint Pty. Ltd.

48 Cambridge Street Collingwood
VIC Australia 3066.
Web: www.sitepoint.com
Email: business@sitepoint.com

ISBN 978-0-9802858-6-4
Printed and bound in Canada

## About the Author

Meri spends her days managing projects at a large multinational, and her evenings writing at Geek | Manager[1] and developing web sites. She loves motorbikes, shooting, tattoos, and going home to beautiful South Africa whenever possible. In her spare time she is an enthusiastic gamer, a novice surfer, and a keen cook.

## About the Expert Reviewers

Kevin Lawver has worked for AOL for thirteen years, building web "stuff" most of that time. As a reward for all that work, AOL lets him work with Ruby on Rails, serve as AOL's AC Representative to the W3C and build lots of fun stuff like ficlets.com. When he's not working or traveling, Kevin blogs with his wife over at http://lawver.net.

Drew McLellan is Senior Web Developer and Director at UK-based web development agency edgeofmyseat.com. He holds the title of Group Lead at the Web Standards Project, and likes to bang on about microformats whenever the opportunity arises. Drew keeps a personal site at allinthehead.com, covering web development issues and themes.

## About the Technical Editor

Toby Somerville is a serial webologist, who caught the programming bug back in 2000. For his sins, he has been a pilot, a blacksmith, a web applications architect, and a freelance web developer. In his spare time he likes to kite buggy and climb stuff.

## About the Technical Director

As Technical Director for SitePoint, Kevin Yank oversees all of its technical publications—books, articles, newsletters, and blogs. He has written over 50 articles for SitePoint, but is best known for his book, *Build Your Own Database Driven Website Using PHP & MySQL*. Kevin lives in Melbourne, Australia, and enjoys performing improvised comedy theater and flying light aircraft.

## About SitePoint

SitePoint specializes in publishing fun, practical, and easy-to-understand content for web professionals. Visit http://www.sitepoint.com/ to access our books, newsletters, articles, and community forums.

---

[1] http://blog.geekmanager.co.uk/

*For my lovely wife, Elly*

# Table of Contents

# Preface

Growing up, I didn't want to be a project manager. Unlike the more popular options of fireman and ballerina (and later doctor and chef), it wasn't as easy to visualize what being a project manager was all about. Since my love was for technology, I studied Computer Science and worked on everything from software engineering through to web development. It was only in the corporate world that I realized why people wanted to be project managers.

Project management is about making things happen.

Good project management is what makes the real work a success. Bad or missing project management can taint and nullify the efforts of even the most talented people. It doesn't matter how brilliant your work is if the project as a whole is twice as expensive as intended, or a year late. This is not to say that the real work isn't important—it is still the core of any project. No project manager can make mediocre work into an awesome end result. But fantastic work can be overlooked if the project management required to deliver the whole isn't there.

Like me, you've probably already realized this. You've worked on a project or two where things went wrong at the project management level. You've figured you could do a better job of it yourself—which is exactly why you bought this book! The good news is that you were right. You can do a good job of the project management. And this book will teach you how.

# Who Should Read This Book?

This book is for anyone who wants to learn enough project management to ensure their projects succeed. You won't become a world authority on the project management discipline, but you will become an effective and efficient project manager. Although some of the examples in this book focus on projects that address technological or systems-related issues—a growing industry in need of skilled project managers!—the book is intended for anyone who needs to manage projects of any sort.

That said, this book won't teach you to manage the construction of the next space shuttle. For very large and very complex projects, you will probably need a few extra and more rigorous tools. You'll find some pointers to such tools in the appendices.

# What's Covered In This Book?

### So What Is Project Management Anyway?

This chapter forms an introduction to the art and science of project management. Here, we talk about the key phases every project goes through and why project management skills are increasingly important today.

### Getting Started

This chapter covers everything from picking the right projects, and working out who needs to be involved, through to kick-starting the project itself.

### Getting the Job Done

In this chapter, we discuss the real meat of any project—planning what needs to be done, executing the work, and controlling the project as a whole to keep things on track.

### Keeping It Smooth

Here, we'll look at communication, collaboration, and how best to deal with change. This chapter is all about the softer side of project management—the skills that make you not just competent, but great.

### Following Through

To wrap up, we'll look at what's involved in successfully finishing off your project and handing over like a superstar.

# The Book's Web Site

Located at http://www.sitepoint.com/books/project1/, the web site that supports this book will give you access to the following facilities.

## Project Management Cheat Sheets

This book explains numerous concepts, processes, and ideas in detail, but on a day-to-day basis, you'll need a quick, easy reference to the key information we've discussed. These downloadable cheat sheets are the answer. Print them, pin them to your wall, and refer to them as you work your way through the project.

### Updates and Errata

No book is error-free, and attentive readers will no doubt spot at least one or two mistakes in this one. The Corrections and Typos[1] page on the book's web site will provide the latest information about known typographical and code errors, and will offer necessary updates for new releases of browsers and related standards.

## The SitePoint Forums

If you'd like to communicate with others about this book, you should join SitePoint's online community.[2] The forums offer an abundance of information above and beyond the solutions in this book, and a lot of fun and experienced business owners hang out there. It's a good way to learn new tricks, get questions answered in a hurry, and just have a good time.

## The SitePoint Newsletters

In addition to books like this one, SitePoint publishes free email newsletters including *The SitePoint Tribune*, *The SitePoint Tech Times*, and *The SitePoint Design View*. Reading them will keep you up to date on the latest news, product releases, trends, tips, and techniques for all aspects of web development. Sign up to one or more SitePoint newsletters at http://www.sitepoint.com/newsletter/.

## Your Feedback

If you can't find an answer through the forums, or if you wish to contact us for any other reason, the best place to write is books@sitepoint.com. We have an email support system set up to track your inquiries, and friendly support staff members who can answer your questions. Suggestions for improvements as well as notices of any mistakes you may find are especially welcome.

---

[1] http://www.sitepoint.com/books/project1/errata.php
[2] http://www.sitepointforums.com/

# Acknowledgments

Thanks to the web community for not only tolerating but embracing me when I broke away from techie topics and started speaking about project management at BarCamps and other events. Thanks to Molly Holzschlag, Maxine Sherrin, and James Edwards for believing I had a book in me, and to Simon Mackie for asking me to write one. Thanks also to Simon, Toby Somerville, and Matty Magain for their editing skills and their understanding of my sometimes insane travel schedule. Thanks to Kevin Lawver and Drew McLellan for all their insight and experience, and for ruthlessly calling me on my management speak.

For my understanding of how to manage both projects and people, I owe thanks to many people. To Michele Hughes, for trusting me with bigger challenges than anyone else would have done. To Joanna Bryson, for letting my artificial intelligence research cross over into project management and helping shape my flexible planning theories. To Paul Cutler, Catherine Horgan, Russ Barrow, Gillian Brownlee, and Emma Jenkins for broadening my horizons and teaching me about the subtleties of the people side of things. To Rob Jones, Sinéad Devine, Rachel Dale, and Julian Padget for equipping me with the skills and rigor to scale up to bigger and more complex projects.

Thanks also to all my friends and family for their love, help and support. In particular my wife Elly, my parents Chris and Paul, my best friends Louis and Liam, the ATG crowd, and all my colleagues both at work and in the geek community.

# Conventions Used In This Book

You'll notice that we've used certain typographic and layout styles throughout this book to signify different types of information. Look out for the following items.

## Tips, Notes, and Warnings

 **Hey, You!**

Tips will give you helpful little pointers.

 **Ahem, Excuse Me ...**

Notes are useful asides that are related—but not critical—to the topic at hand. Think of them as extra tidbits of information.

 **Make Sure You Always ...**

... pay attention to these important points.

 **Watch Out!**

Warnings will highlight any gotchas that are likely to trip you up along the way.

# 1

# So What Is
# Project Management Anyway?

We've all been there: the project seems to be going along fine, although if you're completely honest you're probably a little behind. You're mentally keeping track of all those little items that you need to make sure get done. Then the client calls with a set of changes. You're excited as you think they're "getting it" and so you get stuck in straight away. A week later, you're dreading the "how's it going" call because you know you have no idea anymore. You're lost amidst all the work. You need project management.

In this chapter, we'll firstly have a look at some definitions of project management, ranging from the official to the rather more informal. We'll then consider the project life cycle and uncover some surprises about which parts matter most.

We'll also see why project management tends to be a subject that many find less than enthralling, and why project management skills are increasingly in demand. Then, we'll discuss what project management *isn't* and see how misusing the tools can lead to complications.

# What Is Project Management?

An official definition of **project management**, courtesy of the Project Management Institute, defines the term as: "the application of knowledge, skills, tools and techniques to project activities to meet project requirements."[1]

A more tangible (but less interesting) description is that project management is *everything you need to make a project happen on time and within budget to deliver the needed scope and quality.*

 **My Definition of Project Management**

My personal definition of project management is that it's the easiest way to look like a superhero without the involvement of radioactive spiders or having questionable parentage.

In order to really get our heads around these definitions, we need to discuss some of the terms. A **project** is distinguished from regular work in that it's a one-time effort to change things in some way. So the creation of a new web site would be a project; ongoing maintenance and minor updates would not.

**Time** and **budget** are familiar terms—perhaps the project is intended to take six weeks and have a budget of $20,000. **Scope** refers to the list of deliverables or features that have been agreed—this is where the scale of the required solution is identified. For instance, creating a new web site for the company may realistically be possible in six weeks, but rewriting all the accounting software isn't. **Quality** is exactly what it says on the tin, but in project-speak, quality may include not only the quality of the finished product, but also the approach. Some industries require that particular quality management approaches be used—for instance, factories producing automotive parts have to meet particular international standards.

---

[1] *PMBOK Guide, 3rd Edition*, Project Management Institute Inc., Pennsylvania, 2004.

These four aspects (time, budget, scope, and quality) make up what's known as the **balance quadrant**, which is pictured in Figure 1.1. The balance quadrant demonstrates the interrelationship between the four aspects and how a change to one aspect will unbalance the quadrant. For instance, an increase in the project's scope will have an impact on the time, the cost, and the quality of the project.[2] In practice, any project decision you or your clients make will have an impact on these four aspects—will it make the project more expensive, take longer, be of lower or higher quality, or affect its scope?

Figure 1.1. The balance quadrant

Essentially, project management is a set of skills and tools that will help you get the project right in every way.

# Understanding the Project Life Cycle

The generic project life cycle is fairly simple—first you start the project (called **Initiating**), then you go on to actually *do* the project (through the **Planning**, **Executing**, and **Controlling** phases, which form a loop), and finally you finish with everyone happy, a strategy for the future in place, and a check in your hand (**Closing**). This process is illustrated in Figure 1.2.

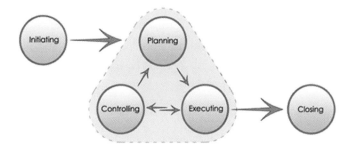

Figure 1.2. The project life cycle

---

[2] You may previously have heard of the project triangle (containing three of those four elements)—essentially, the balance quadrant is a real-world version of that concept. For more on the project triangle, see http://en.wikipedia.org/wiki/Project_triangle/.

In the coming chapters, we'll look into each phase in more detail. Much of the work required in these phases will be very familiar to you—after all, you've been successfully getting work done already! The real message of the project life cycle, though, is that the areas that take the most time are not necessarily the most important.

Most people spend most of the project time working in the Executing and Controlling phases—actually doing the tasks, building the product, and making sure everything is on track. Of course, this work is hugely valuable—without it, there wouldn't be much point starting the project at all—but these phases aren't typically where the success or failure of a project is dictated. That happens in the other three phases—Initiating, Planning, and Closing—which makes them the most important phases of all.

But why are Initiating, Planning, and Closing so important? The way to think about this is to imagine the repercussions if these phases were completed badly or even ignored completely.

## Failure to Launch ... or Land

If Initiating isn't done right, you often end up in a situation where the project team members have very different ideas about the project's purpose, and eventually disagree about the point at which the project is really finished. If you think success is a good design and a series of static pages, but the customers' number one requirement is "first result on Google," you could deliver a great product that they view as a failure. The Initiating phase provides an opportunity to ensure that everyone in the team is on the same page from the start, and that misconceptions and conflicts are addressed, rather than left to fester. Good initiation will also ensure that you identify all the project **stakeholders** (all those who are involved, interested in, or affected by the project) up-front, which avoids the likelihood that they'll pop up at inopportune moments during the project!

## Example 1.1. Knowing Your Stakeholders

I once worked on a project that was meant to deliver a new software program to a team that collected data from different supermarkets and turned it into reports. The designer was intent on making the program as user-friendly as possible, which was a laudable aim, but sadly his definition of usable was significantly different from that of the actual *users*!

The designer had focused on making the software so simple that anyone could use it—even a novice—when in fact only a very limited number of data-entry clerks were going to use it. They were rather upset when they discovered they weren't to be consulted, and quite disgruntled when they were presented with a system that, it appeared, would make their work take four times longer than before!

The reality was that, for them, speed was the most important factor. Ignoring these stakeholders led to disastrous consequences for the project—the entire design was scrapped and six months' work had to be redone. Of course, this time, the data-entry clerks were properly involved in the design process!

Failing in the Planning phase can be equally disastrous for your project. If you don't plan at all, how will you know what you should be doing next? Similarly, planning once at the beginning of the project, and expecting just to be able to follow that plan, is both wonderfully naïve and seriously dangerous. Unless you're far more prescient than the rest of us, it's incredibly difficult to plan what should be done on Tuesday three months from now.

The best planning approach tends to be one that lets you plan the project's immediate future in detail, and plan tasks that lie further out at a higher level. This is known as the **rolling wave** approach to planning. The deliverables for the next three to four weeks are broken down into sections, so that it's possible to keep track of the project's progress on a day-to-day basis. Anything further off than a month is left unplanned, as a high-level deliverable, so that you can keeping an eye on what lies ahead without becoming overly focused on the minute details.

Not paying proper attention to the closure of your project can be just as problematic as poor initiating or planning. If you think your project is finished when you finish building the product, then you're in for a nasty surprise: what I call zombie stakeholders, who keep coming back, again and again, asking for "just one more change," or insisting that you fix remaining bugs and issues that they find. Part of finishing a project with excellence is making sure that the product you've built has a future.

If you're inclined to pick up support contracts for all the projects you implement, you need to execute the Closing phase properly—ad hoc arrangements will always come back to bite you later. If you intend to hand over the future maintenance and support of the product to someone else—perhaps a person who's internal to your customer's organization—then, again, this needs care. Just throwing the work over the fence to them and wandering off to your next project will almost guarantee dissatisfaction on one side or the other eventually.

# Negative Perceptions of Project Management

Some unfortunate misperceptions make project management rate on most people's list of preferred activities somewhere between putting the garbage out and deliberately stubbing their big toes—that is, somewhere between tedious and painful.

## It's Boring

The first misperception is that project management is an incredibly boring distraction from "real work." Whatever your current vocation, you're probably engaged in it because you enjoy it, and are good at it. Taking time away from what you normally do to focus on project management just doesn't feel right.

The reality, though, is that without an appropriate focus on project management, all that real work could be for nothing—what you build might be beautiful, but it won't help anyone if it's not what the customer needed, costs twice as much as planned, or is completed a month late.

So, at the very worst, we should agree that project management is a necessary evil. By the end of this book, I hope to convince you that it is also an incredibly useful skillset both inside and outside of work, and can really help you showcase your other abilities.

# It Takes Too Long

The second misperception that drives people's view of project management is that it takes a huge amount of time. This *can* be true. If you try to do everything that traditional project management demands, you can certainly feel like managing your projects is turning into a full-time job.

What is needed is a balance between the science of project management (what you're told you *should* do) and the art of project management (what you actually *need* to do). In this book, we'll focus on the minimalist side of the art: the judicious application of the right tools in the right situations is the hallmark of a great project manager.

# It's Too Hard

The other negative perception of project management is that it's just plain difficult. Personally, I believe that anyone can pick up project management skills and apply them in a useful manner. I also believe that most people have already mastered more difficult disciplines in their current jobs. Why, then, is project management so scary?

One reason is that project management is talked about far less than other topics. Although it's easy to argue that most people will need to manage a project of some sort at some point in their lives, it's still not an area that's generally covered at school or even at college.

Another reason for the perception that project management is so difficult is that many project management tools are complicated! The first time I opened Microsoft Project I was completely perplexed—what was I meant to be doing? Eventually I borrowed someone else's existing project plan and adapted it, slowly learning the quirks of the software. Since then, the number of project documents I've seen written in Excel, PowerPoint, or even text files continues to convince me that many project management tools are just too complex for most people.

Project management can also be a world of its own, complete with acronyms, jargon, slang, and in-jokes. In fact, some project managers rely on this, overusing the terminology to make their jobs seem more mystical. Others just enjoy the fact that project management seems to have created a whole new category of Dilbert cartoons and try not to imitate them too much.

The approaches and tools that we'll cover in the upcoming chapters are all simple to understand and easy to apply. You may find that you're flexing different muscles than you do in your normal day-to-day work, but equally you'll feel the benefit of that increased strength in your regular activities as well. More importantly, you'll gain a skillset that is increasingly important in today's world.

# What Project Management Isn't

We've talked a lot already about what project management *is*; now we need to consider some of the things for which it's often mistaken. The reason we're addressing this up-front is that the misuse of project management tools for other purposes is one of the main reasons for those negative perceptions we discussed earlier.

Firstly, *project management is not personal productivity*. This is an easy mistake to make, however. Most folks' early experience with project management is on smaller projects on which they're doing most of the work themselves. It's easy to start treating the project schedule as your diary, the task list as your to-do list. But as soon as you add anyone else to the project, be it a client who wants to understand the time line or a colleague helping out with some of the work, this approach starts to cause problems.

If you make your project management tools double as personal productivity tools, you'll almost certainly be including far too much detail. Keep a clean line between what you need for yourself personally, and what the project needs. This way, when you have slightly larger projects with more people involved, your tools will scale.

Secondly, *project management is not people management*. This may seem obvious, but I'm always surprised by the number of managers I meet who seem to think that they can manage their people in the same way they do a project. People are infinitely more complex than your average project. There are also some amazing books out there about people management—if you're interested, some resources are supplied in Appendix B.

We'll talk later on about how to manage the involvement of people in your project, but if you have people reporting to you, and you're responsible for their careers, the references in Appendix B can tell you a lot more about how to keep them productive and happy than can any book on project management.

Thirdly, *project management is not operations or service management.* The challenges and best practices for ongoing day-to-day operations are very different from those involved in project management. An incident in a live system has to be dealt with in a very different way from an issue on your project. Again, a wealth of information is available that details the best approach to operations management—covering everything from ITIL (Information Technology Infrastructure Library) through to anecdotes about how Google deals with machine burnout in its vast array of indexing computers.

# Why You Need PM Skills

Projects are an increasing feature of modern work. Once, workers performed the same set of tasks, day after day, focusing on getting more of the same done as quickly and efficiently as possible. Today, one of the few constants is that the work you do today will be different from what you do tomorrow. For many, our jobs consist of an ongoing stream of new projects, new technologies, and new challenges.

This is particularly true in our modern world, where technology is an intrinsic part of almost any business. These days, it's hard to imagine a company that could survive without telephones, email, computers, and handhelds. It's even harder to imagine technology staying the same for more than a few years—at the most!

We also face changing expectations among our clients and business partners. Today, there's much more of an expectation that you will deliver not just an isolated product, but a solution to a business problem. Delivering that full solution requires a broader skillset than was traditionally expected.

## What's In It for Me?

So, how will project management help you? What will it give you that you don't already have?

First and foremost, developing your project management skills will empower you to deliver the real solution that your customers and clients want. You'll be able to manage everything, from start to finish—including their involvement—in a much more effective manner.

Secondly, investing some time in project management will make everything else run more smoothly. In fact, you'll hopefully find that instead of detracting from the real work, your new-found project management skills will allow you more time to focus on the work that you really enjoy, by making managing the process aspects of your job much less stressful. You never know—project management might even become the work that you love best!

Thirdly, project management is one of those valuable transferable skills that careers advisors are always so keen on. Wherever you see your career going, there aren't a lot of places in which project management wouldn't be a bonus. If you find that you like it enough to want to make it the focus of your career, you might consider investing in professional qualifications.

# The Underlying Principles of Project Management

Before we move to look at the methods, practices, and tools of project management, let's first take some time to think about some underlying principles. These are fundamental truths—and while ignoring them won't necessarily spell disaster for your project, it can greatly diminish your chances of success.

## Doing PM Right Is an Investment In Making the "Real Work" Matter

It can be easy to see project management as a function that's all overhead and no return. This is especially true when you first start to make use of the approaches and practices we've discussed so far—they can feel a little alien. But you can rest assured that your project management work will become much easier with practice.

Even if project management really was as boring, tedious, and difficult as some people assume it to be, it would still be worth doing. The reason I believe this point to be fundamentally true is that without decent project management, the value of everything else you do can be negated. Failing to invest in project management on the basis that the funds can be better spent in other areas of the project (for instance, on employing more team members to do the real work) can seem like a good idea, but it leaves the project team open to a much greater risk of delivering late, over-spending, or creating a product that's not up to scratch or in line with what the customer wants. Countless things can go wrong on any project, and that's why project management is an essential function.

Project management is an investment in getting it right—a bit like making sure that the foundations and walls of a building are strong before you start the intricate carving on the front door. Setting up your project to succeed, and adhering to the processes that will keep it on track, can determine whether all the real work pays off in the end or not.

## People Problems Can't Be Solved with Software

With all the modern technology now at our disposal, many of us like to believe that we can heal the world's problems with appropriate application of hardware and software. Perhaps ending world hunger is a little beyond our abilities, but what about getting teams to work well together? Surely *that* can be solved with the judicious introduction of a nice web application?

Sadly, people are a lot more complex, and can seem more irrational, than we like to believe. We can't solve people problems with software—the best we can hope to achieve is to refocus some of the teams' anger and resentment onto the tool that you introduce.

When you start work on a new project, look at the situation and identify the people and the process problems separately. Then, look at how you can address the people problems *before* you begin to try to find a solution to the process problems. The good news is that a lot of the art of project management is about solving people problems. We'll be talking about this a great deal in the coming chapters—especially in Chapter 4, which focuses on good communication and collaboration.

Of course, addressing people problems isn't just something that you need to do at the start of a project. You'll need to monitor your team and the people your project affects as the project progresses, and address issues as they arise. When something goes wrong, look for people problems first. The role of the project manager is to make sure that the different parties' viewpoints are heard, and that everyone agrees to respect the course of action chosen, even if, as individuals, they would have made a different decision.

## If it Doesn't Add Value, it Won't Get Done

As you become more of a project manager, you'll find you have a mile-long list of things you'd like the team to do: track exactly how much time team members spend coding each new feature, detail exactly which budget element the yesterday's pizza order should be charged to, update the plan to show the team's progress every day, keep logs of how accurate the time estimates were, and so on.

There are myriad examples of things that would make your life as a project manager *much* easier if only everyone would play ball. But the reality is that, if an item helps only you, rather than benefiting the whole project team, it will be very difficult to convince anyone else to complete that task, since they'll see no benefit in doing so. No one likes doing pointless work (and we all define "pointless" from our own personal perspectives), and you can be assured that your team members will indicate to you whether a task you've asked them to do has any value.

If a task doesn't have value, don't ask your mean members to do it. Your project team contains brilliant people—whether they're designers or developers, carpenters or plumbers—and you should only take their time away from doing what they're best at when it's absolutely necessary. Make sure that everything you ask your team to do adds value to the project at both an individual and collective level.

 **Perceived Value Versus Real Value**

Sometimes the reason why your team members can't see value in a task is simply that you haven't explained the point of a particular process. Be on the lookout for tasks that provide value to both the individual and the project, but the team hasn't realized this. It's up to you to make sure the team members understand the value of the work they're doing.

## The Best Tool Is the One that Works and Gets Used

If I had a dollar for every time someone emailed me a link to a new Web 2.0 project management tool, my house would even more crammed with SciFi DVD box sets than it is now. There are literally thousands of tools out there—so many, in fact, that selecting one to use on a project can become an overwhelming task.

Fortunately, choosing the right project management tool is much less of an individual decision than you might expect. After all, project management is about in-process communication—you'll need to be able to share the project plan, and have everyone update the issue list and collaborate on the project documentation. And whatever tool you use, you'll want the entire team to adopt it enthusiastically. These requirements will severely—and quite helpfully—limit the tools that you can consider using.

That's why some organizations run their entire project management process through Excel or Powerpoint.[3] It's also why those managing house renovation projects will display a board or flipchart that lists the current priorities in a spot where every person who enters the house will see it.

The best tool is often dictated by the software or tracking techniques that the members of the team are comfortable using—which is why tools that appear to have all the right features can fail abysmally. You'd be surprised by the number of project managers who didn't realize their clients or team members couldn't open the plan they'd compiled in Microsoft Project until the third set of delays that resulted the fact that no one could see the schedule.

When you're choosing project management tools, make sure that you're picking not only one that's functional—it will get the job done—but one that will be adopted wholeheartedly by all the people involved in the project.

To help you understand what you really need, as well as what your options are, we'll be discussing the sorts of tools and best practices that are useful in each project phase. In Appendix A, you'll find some pointers to specific software that you can consider.

---

[3] No, really, I've actually seen an entire project run through PowerPoint. I have the emotional scars to prove it!

# The Best Way to Communicate Is the Way That Gets You Heard

This point closely echoes the previous one. Choosing the right form, method, and content for your communication is hugely important to your project's success. Chapter 4 is dedicated to a discussion of your options, but the underlying communications principle is that you should *choose the approach that will actually get you heard.*

Communication is an area in which it's particularly important to understand organizational culture—which statement is really just management speak for the saying, "When in Rome, do as the Romans do." If your, or your client's, company is the kind of environment where emails are ignored and face-to-face meetings are the only way to make decisions, you need to make sure you have face-to-face meetings. Likewise, if items are agreed to in meetings but aren't binding until someone sends out the meeting minutes, then it's of paramount importance that you send the minutes of your meetings promptly, and that you include people's names against the action steps.

Even if you agree as a team, for instance, that project status updates will be sent out weekly, over email, don't take it for granted that they're being read. Silence can easily be interpreted as tacit agreement, but it can also mean, "Sorry, this project rates on my priority list somewhere below watching the football and reading comics online." Ask the people you're trying to communicate with whether your communication is actually working—don't just keep doing what you're doing, and risk having everything to explode at a later date.

# Choosing the Right Tools and Processes Is the PM's Most Important Job

As you've probably gathered from our discussions of the other underlying principles at play in the world of project management, as the project manager, you'll need to make a lot of choices: which tools to use, how to communicate with your team and your clients, and how best to design your work processes—among other things! Making the right decisions about which processes and tools you'll use is going to be your most important job as a project manager.

Anyone can write a project plan or update an issue list. On the other hand, writing a project plan that everyone will actually follow, or creating an issue list management process that people will actually use, are separate challenges. Project management isn't about going it alone and creating all the artifacts (the plans, schedules, issue lists, status updates, and so on) by yourself. It's about running the project; those artifacts should be no more—or less—than useful and effective by-products of a project that's going well.

Choosing or designing the right processes and finding the tools to support them is going to be your biggest challenge as a project manager. Don't worry, you'll have plenty of help—Appendix A is devoted to an exploration of various project management tools, and in each of the coming chapters, we'll discuss the best practices for the given project phase. There's also a wealth of information on the Web, as Appendix B reveals, and probably at least some prior experience in your own organization.

Don't think of any of the decisions you make about the project as being trivial. Understand the importance and the implications of each choice, and be prepared to change when something isn't working well. Take responsibility not only for introducing the tools, but also for marshaling their adoption. And above all, watch out for signs of a deeper problem—the times when no extra features or better performance will improve the adoption of a given tool or approach, because the underlying processes are broken. Equally, look for opportunities or fluctuations—tools that really helped a new team that hadn't gelled at the beginning of the project could become obsolete as their collaboration improves.

## Summary

Now that we've talked about what project management is (and isn't!), discussed the project life cycle, and identified why gaining project management skills is going to make you a superstar, we need to get started!

In the next chapter, we'll look at how to identify the best projects and get them off to a running start.

Chapter

# 2

# Getting Started

You've already got an understanding of the basic project life cycle, and we've just talked through some of the underlying principles of project management. But I bet you're itching to actually *do* something. In this chapter, we'll talk about the work that comes *before* the project life cycle—finding possible projects, working out which projects are worth pursuing, and getting to know the different groups of people who will be involved in any project. Finally, we'll discuss the process of actually initiating a project.

In each of the sections that follow, you'll find a discussion of what the process is and why it matters, followed by tools and best practices that will help you get your project off to a flying start.

## Discovery: Finding the Projects

Projects don't just spring from nowhere. Although many project managers only get involved when it's already been decided that a project will be undertaken to achieve some end, there is, of course, a phase before this: discovery. **Discovery** is the process by which the organization reviews the available opportunities and decides which of them will become projects in due course.

Ideally, the discovery process should ensure that the best opportunities are pursued—not just those that were mentioned first, or those that have the loudest supporters. Where this process is undertaken, it's usually combined with some sort of **portfolio planning** through which the potential projects are matched against the resources or capabilities of the organization itself. The eventual result is a list of projects that are truly the top priorities.

The sad reality is that in many cases, there's either no process at all for discovery and portfolio planning, or the process that's in place doesn't result in the selection of projects that will deliver the most value. It's also true that as a project manager, your influence may be very limited at this stage—after all, in many cases, you won't even know about the potential projects until one is assigned to you!

However, understanding what has been discovered, and how the project that you're managing came to be started, is very important. It can tell you whether the project is truly of high value to the organization for which you're working (either as an employee, contractor, or service provider) or whether its potential value still needs to be ascertained. It may also give you early insight into the complexities you might have to face during the project.

If you find that little or no discovery work has been done, don't despair—do it yourself! Find out why people in the organization think your project is important. Understand what they're expecting the project to deliver—try to focus on what it means to them, not the nuts and bolts of what will be built. If their answers suggest that they don't think the project matters, find out where they think the time and effort would be better spent.

Your first instinct will be to protect your project, but you might find an opportunity for another project that will deliver even more value. Even if you don't end up jettisoning the original project and taking on the new one instead, bringing it to the attention of the stakeholders within the organization will make you stand out as a project manager who really cares about the good of the company, not just your own projects.

## Example 2.1. Choosing the Wrong Options

Imagine there's a team at a company you're working with that deals with customer orders. The team members have identified a number of opportunities:

**Remove manual work from current processes.**
Many in the team feel that they spend almost all their time shuffling paper, rather than actually dealing with the customers.

**Speed up inventory checking.**
When a customer places an order, the team members have to call up the inventory team to find out whether the goods are in stock or not. Making this process faster would improve their efficiency greatly.

**Improve tracking of customer orders, queries, and complaints.**
Currently, all tracking of customer interactions is done manually. There's actually one person in the team whose full-time job is collecting the information and putting it in an Excel spreadsheet!

**Allow customers to interact in more ways.**
A number of customers have signalled that they'd like to be able to email the team as a whole, or to input queries and complaints online.

As you might have guessed, the opportunities above are ordered in terms of importance. The team feels that reducing their manual work is most important, with the inventory tracking improvements and customer tracking automation coming a close second. Once these fundamental issues have been fixed, the team feels that it can start work on items that will really benefit the customer—introducing a web site and email addresses so they can log orders, queries, and so on.

When people from elsewhere in the organization get involved, however, they get very focused on the web site for the customers. Marketing can see that this will be a real selling point and the sales teams think that it will delight their contacts. They don't realize that in order for the customer web site to be successful, the team needs to have all the other opportunities addressed first.

The first you know about any of this, however, is when you're brought in to build the new customer web site. You get started working on it, but are finding that the people from the team who deal with the orders are very difficult to work with: they won't answer questions clearly, don't turn up to meetings that you've organized, and don't answer emails unless they're reminded to again and again. You're sensing hostility, but you have no idea why—you've only been there a week. Surely you can't have offended them already?

You get in touch with some of the IT guys that you know from the last project you worked on for this company and ask them what's up. They explain about the other projects that this team identified … and that the team actually thought those other projects were more important. However, someone in the marketing team, having heard about the possibility of the web site being developed, promised one of the big customers that it would be ready soon, so management decided to prioritize this project over the improvement of the systems.

Now you understand why the team is so unresponsive! They're upset because their own needs have been ignored, and now you're working on the project that they've been forced into prematurely.

At this point, it can be very easy to get depressed or start panicking. What if the team continues to sabotage the project and you get blamed when it isn't delivered? You don't have the power to go back and work on the project they really wanted to happen, so perhaps you should just give up now …

The point, though, is that now you *understand* what was causing the team to be unhelpful and unresponsive. Armed with that knowledge, you can do something about it!

As we've already discussed, often the project manager won't be involved in deciding which projects will be undertaken. In this particular situation, however, you can try to mitigate some of the impacts of the web site project being prioritized over that of updating the existing systems.

Firstly, you have a discussion with Pamela, the team member who's been the main cause of friction so far. You explain that you understand there were originally other projects on the cards, and ask her to clarify for you what they would have entailed.

As she talks, you realize that some of the elements of the existing manual process are going to be problematic for your project as well—for instance, it won't be possible to determine whether or not an item is in stock without someone making a phone call.

In this particular example, there's an obvious route forward—help to identify the modernizations of the existing system that are required for the web site project to be a real success. Then push either for these to be brought into the scope of your own project, or for a separate team to be set up to deal with those issues in parallel.

However, even if you won't be able to influence the organization to work on the productivity improvements as well as the site, just having spoken to Pamela seems to have improved relations immensely. She commented that you were the first one of the "techie guys" who had taken the time to really understand why the team is so frustrated. She has started responding to your queries and emails and even seems to have told the rest of the team that they should help you out as well.

The point is that without understanding where your project's roots lie, you're flying blind. By investing some time to find out a little more about how the discovery work was or wasn't done, and how the decisions were made, you can gain a valuable insight into the challenges you might face, day to day, on the project. This approach can also give you an early warning of any office politics that might make your life difficult!

# Picking the Best Projects

Choosing the best projects to work on involves a three-step process:

1. Identify the opportunities.
2. Compare the opportunities.
3. Rank them and decide which to undertake.

## Identifying the Opportunities

There are many approaches to identifying opportunities, some of which are more sophisticated than others, so let's start by considering some of the basic tools that you'll probably already have come across.

The most obvious option is a brainstorm. Get people in the organization together, and ask them to think of anything that annoys them, anything that could be done better, or things that aren't being done yet that could be started.

 **The Stop, Start, Continue Approach**

One model that you can use to get people to focus called Stop, Start, Continue. Here, you essentially ask the people in the room to name one task they want the organization to stop doing, one task that it should start doing, and one task that it should continue to do.

If it's obvious that a particular business process or set of processes is causing a lot of pain, manual work, or rework in the organization, it might be worth charting that process. You can do this using any tool—from the good old marker and whiteboard, through to bespoke process-flow mapping tools or UML diagrams.[1]

Once you have drawn out the business process, look at each step and ask, "Why do we do this?" If there isn't a good reason to take the step, remove it! If the step is necessary but could be done more intelligently, ask how. If the question of what needs to change isn't answered easily, a project to fully investigate the options and create a solution could spring from your analysis.

---

### Example 2.2. Innovate or Improve

One example of the need for innovation is made clear by the anecdote about an early 20th-century buggy whip manufacturer. The organization was focused on making whips (used on horses that drew buggies and carts) faster, cheaper, and better … at a time when horse-drawn carts were rapidly being replaced by motor cars. Making the buggy whip cheaper was not going to increase sales, since price was not the problem.

---

[1] **UML** stands for Unified Modeling Language, and constitutes a set of standard formats for creating flow diagrams of processes, data, etc. UML tends to be popular with usability professionals and software engineers. As always, think carefully about the tools you choose—they need to be understandable and accessible to everyone involved.

Remember, though, that sometimes the opportunities that are the biggest—the projects that will make a huge difference to the business—might be those that *don't* represent incremental improvements. In many cases, the real way to make a difference may be to realize that there's a completely new direction to take, product to focus on, or way to operate.

## Comparing the Opportunities

Once you have a list of opportunities that could be addressed, you then need to work out which is the most important. You might want to start by identifying what benefit would be generated if the process was fixed, the gap was filled, or the new service was created. Would it reduce the amount of work for someone? Make the company more money? Bring in new customers? Reduce risk in some way?

Typically, the reasons why a company decides to approach an opportunity are one—or a combination—of the following benefits:

- to increase income (higher sales, new market, new service)
- to decrease costs (make it cheaper, faster, lower inventory)
- to improve productivity (same work done with less time/cost/people)
- to reduce risk (increase tax compliance, improve audit score)

Once you've identified what the benefit of each project is, you need to work out how big that benefit will be. Ideally, you'll want to be able to measure the benefit in numbers somehow—whether it's that someone can get 50% more invoices posted, that sales increase by $50,000, that widgets now cost only ten cents, or that your accountants smile for the first time in living memory.

 **What's the Problem?**

At this stage, you're still comparing the opportunities, *not* the projects! Think of problems and gaps at this stage—we'll be looking at the solutions (projects) soon enough.

Later on in this chapter, one of the discovery tools we'll look at is **value creation**—an approach to working out the value that will be delivered by a project.

# Ranking and Choosing Opportunities to Pursue

Now that you have an idea of the available opportunities, and how much of a benefit could be gained from addressing them, you need to work out which one to tackle. You may have uncovered an opportunity that's so big that you feel it's imperative to go ahead and deal with it immediately. More likely, however, is the eventuality that you'll have a number of options, and will need to decide which is the most important.

First, rank the opportunities in order of their potential benefits. Second, work out what a project might entail in very, very rough detail—literally just a sentence or two describing how you'd go about solving the problem. If you have no clue, the project may well focus on researching and finding a solution that can, ultimately, be implemented!

For instance, if we think back to our earlier case study, the problems had already been ranked in the order that was most important to the customer service organization. Their focus was cost saving and productivity. It was when the marketing folks (who are more focused on increasing sales) got involved that the equation changed, as they were interested in the increased income.

In this situation, we might rank the opportunities available through a project in terms of the number of areas each would affect. To do so, we could use a matrix like the one in Table 2.1.

Ideally, the next step would be to quantify the benefit by working out the numbers. In the case of a clear cost saving, assigning a figure is easy. If you predict that reducing paperwork will mean a monthly saving of the funds currently spent on paper, printers, photocopiers, and so on, you can simply total those numbers. When you start to predict increased sales and productivity improvements, however, the calculations become fuzzier. Don't get hung up on representing everything in cash terms; instead, express the benefit as clearly as possible, so you can get it in front of the right people to have a decision made about the project.

## Table 2.1. Ranking and Roughing Out Opportunities and Benefits

| Opportunity | Project | Benefit |
| --- | --- | --- |
| Remove manual work from current processes. | Combine process analysis (to remove manual steps) and automation. | Productivity improvement; cost reduction |
| Speed up inventory checking. | Connect inventory system with existing customer order system. | Productivity improvement |
| Improve tracking of customer orders, queries, and complaints. | Develop additional functionality in the existing customer order system to accommodate queries and complaints tracking. | Productivity improvement; increased income (from increased customer satisfaction) |
| Allow customers to interact in more ways. | Introduce customer service web site and email address. | Increased income |

Next, try to rank the projects in terms of which are easier or cheaper to complete. Depending on your situation, the questions of ease and affordability may be of greater or lesser importance. If people within your organization could be assigned to a given project, you're probably more concerned with how quickly they could make a difference. On the other hand, if you'd have to pay a third party to come in and deal with the project, the project's cost may be a bigger issue.

Having worked out where the greatest benefit can be gained for the lowest cost, you can, in collaboration with the relevant stakeholders, pick a project or two to proceed with.

### It's Only a Rule of Thumb

Don't forget that at this point, all you have are initial estimates. You haven't spent a great deal of time making sure that the potential benefits and projected costs are really accurate.

This is a "rule of thumb" type tool—in the project Initiation phase, you should make sure that both the cost and benefit sides of the equation are investigated and validated. If you find that an element of the project is considerably different than you'd predicted, you might even come back to the discovery phase and pick a different project to work on.

**Is the Best Project for the Organization the Best for You?**

This process is focused on finding the best projects for the organization. As an external contractor or service provider, you also need to care about the benefits your business will gain from the projects you work on.

You might also want to conduct a similar comparison of the projects you have the option of undertaking—across all your clients—and picking the ones most likely to benefit your own organization. The process will be the same, but some of the considerations might be different. For example, you might choose to undertake a project that will make less profit, but has strong potential to lead to more work in future. You should invest as much energy in choosing the right projects for yourself as you do in helping your clients select the best projects for their own needs.

# Spotting Bad Projects

As we've already discussed, many project managers aren't involved in the discovery phase, where good projects are selected. As a result, an ability to spot the signs of a bad project is a valuable skill for the project manager to develop.

First of all, let's think about some hallmarks of *good* projects:

- They deliver *big benefits*, with defined metrics that specify the size of those benefits.

- They're *important to the future* of the organization (or, in management speak, they're "strategically important").

- *Sufficient resources* are invested in them.

- They have *supporters* within the organization.

We'll talk more about the kinds of supporters you need, and the importance of having a sponsor for your project, later in this chapter.

The hallmarks of a bad project contrast rather predictably with those outlined above:

■ Projects for which no one has really identified the business benefit, or for which the closest you can get to a cost estimate is someone waving their hands in a the-size-of-the-monster-catfish-I-caught-last-summer type gesture are dangerous.

■ Projects that focus too heavily on the present and neglect the future are dangerous. Think of the buggy whip manufacturer investing in making his production lines faster and cheaper, rather than realizing that a change in direction was needed.

■ Insufficient—or nonexistent—resource investments in a project are another warning sign that you should beware of. Projects without budgets, people, or equipment are risky from the outset.

■ Projects that are being undertaken even though only a few people in the organization believe that they should be completed are the most dangerous of all. These kinds of projects quickly start to feel like everyone's just standing around watching, and waiting for you to slip up and prove them right.

### Beware of Focusing In the Wrong Place

Today's technology is very advanced, and as a consequence, our options seem limitless. It's rare that tasks aren't attempted because they're viewed as being impossible. In fact, quite the opposite is true—organizations often choose the unlikeliest paths, optimistically believing that their rough plans will all come right in the end.

I have nothing against optimism, but personally, I like to have the odds stacked in my favor! Making sure that you're focused on the real reasons for completing the project, rather than on what's technically possible, is imperative. A benefit-focused approach also often makes the difference between a fantastic project manager (who achieves what the organization *needs*) and a mediocre project manager (who does what's asked, but doesn't work out if that's what's best).

Why would any of these projects survive, you ask? Well, the reality is that they won't! The reason that they get started in the first place is that the people creating the project aren't really sure about what they're trying to achieve. Helping them to define the business benefit is usually the first step to fixing this issue—as soon as they realize how important the project is, dedicating the required investment into resources is an obvious step to take. Supporters also flock to important projects (so much so that you might actually be overwhelmed). Making sure that the work is aligned with the strategic objectives of the company is what those high-level sponsors are good at.

## Project, or Day–by–day Improvement?

The other question that needs to be worked out during the discovery phase is whether a project is really needed at all. Although a project is, at its simplest, just a one-time piece of work, in practice, most organizations also have guidelines that describe what's seen to constitute a project, and what's regarded as merely a minor change or fix.

As an example, the rule of thumb in many companies is, "if the job needs at least one full-time staff member for two weeks (or the equivalent), then it's a project." The important issue here is the size of the effort—if you're going to have two people working full-time for a week, or four people working at 25% of capacity for two weeks, those staff hours all reflect the same amount of effort. A job that will take one person a day or two, by contrast, would not be treated as a real project.

Work that's routine or ongoing is never a project. The management speak for this kind of work tends to involved words like "operational excellence" or "continuous improvement," which are both really just corporate ways of saying "being better at what we do every day." Sometimes, a project will be undertaken to introduce a capability that will make the day-to-day work more efficient and productive—for instance, updating the systems that are used, or introducing new business processes such as problem, change, and incident management.

Very small pieces of work, or mini-projects, may well be absorbed into the normal day-to-day work. This approach can blur the lines between project work and normal operations for many people. It's worth understanding how the organizations you're working with distinguish projects from regular work, and thinking about the impact this may have on the projects you're leading.

If some of the people involved in your projects usually just work on day-to-day operational tasks, they may be completely unfamiliar with a project-based style of work. You might need to meet with them separately to explain project management, clarify your role as the project manager, and illustrate how the project will be run.

### Setting Expectations and Priorities

You might also need to set expectations more explicitly around deadlines and priorities—it can be hard for individuals to prioritize project work over day-to-day operational tasks unless they've been told this is the right attitude to take.

Again, this isn't a huge issue, but you should be aware of it. When you're very used to completing project-based work, it can be easy to forget how the other half lives!

# Discovery Tools and Practices

The full range of tools and practices that can be useful in discovering projects within an organization would include:

- idea elicitation
- portfolio management
- organization building
- resource planning

On their own, the discussion of these tools could easily warrant a separate book, so I'm going to focus on the tools and practices you're most likely to need as a project manager who gets involved once the decision to undertake the project has already been made: project proposals and value creation.

## Project Proposals

**Project proposals** are simple, short (usually single-page) documents that outline the potential project, provide brief background information, identify the value of undertaking the project, and give a very rough estimate of the resources (budget, people, time) that would be required to deliver the project.[2] Ideally, a project proposal is collected for each of the possible projects, and from this pool, the projects that are determined to have the potential to deliver the greatest benefit to the organization are chosen. The project proposal is a document that illustrates the value of completing the project and recommending that the project be resourced.

---

[2] Project proposals are sometimes called project request documents (PRDs) or project charters, though the latter indicates a little more finality and is more like the project initiation document we'll talk about later in this chapter.

Now, this may sound good, but have you spotted the big warning sign yet? These proposals are the first indication to management of what the project will be, and what it will deliver. They even include rough estimates of how long the project will take, how much it will cost, and how many people will need to be assigned to it. Yet minimal effort is invested in getting these estimates right—the project doesn't exist yet, so no one's actually working on it! Of course it would be unrealistic to expect anything else, so really this is just a caveat we all need to be aware of.

We've already identified that project proposals are fundamentally flawed, so why am I advocating them? Well, what would be worse than a flawed project proposal? It would be worse to have nothing at all! At least if you have a proposal, you have documentation that represents the foundations of a contract between the project team, the customer, and management. Without it, you have to guess the expectations of each group—clearly an unenviable task unless your telepathic skills have been improving recently!

But what can you do if there isn't even a project proposal, and you're faced with amorphous, hand-waving descriptions of what the project is meant to be? This is the beauty of the project proposal—you can have a proposal written retrospectively, even if the decision to go ahead with the project has already been made. Some companies and freelancers use a very similar template to form the basis of quotes.

Once the project proposal is written—by you, or by someone else—what can it give us? There are three key pieces of information that project managers will want to obtain from the project proposal:

1. **Understand the project's background.**
    What problem does the problem solve? What process does it affect?

2. **Gain a clear explanation of the business value that the project will deliver.**
    Why is the project important to the organization?

3. **Ascertain the expectations of the project's timing, personnel, and budget.**
    If, from the outset, you can see that the project is hopelessly underfunded, or that the delivery date is wildly optimistic, it will be better to deal with these concerns up-front rather than coming to them later, when your wish to change these factors may be perceived as an attempt to renege on the initial project agreement.

Project proposals can also help us to identify assumptions and constraints. Remember the four opportunities we discussed earlier, in the example in the section called "Discovery: Finding the Projects"? When we go back to write project proposals for each of those opportunities, it'll become obvious that implementing a customer web site without fixing the manual processing, inventory, and call-tracking issues isn't sensible.

The scope of the project can then be expanded to include a complete customer relationship management (CRM) solution. This way, the operational team will only need to use one system to manage *all* of the customer interactions, and the task of optimizing the business processes can become part of your project.

## Value Creation

Delivering value is the *only* real reason to undertake a project. Whether you're increasing the monetary value of your home by adding an extension, or increasing the productivity of a team by making computer systems easier to use, there should always be a clear benefit to completing the project.

One of the most common issues that causes misunderstandings between business people and technical people is that they talk about value in different ways. For example, a technical team member might be talking about load-balancing the servers and introducing new quad-core processors while the business person stares at her, perplexed. When she's asked to elucidate, the techie starts trying to explain how it all works, so that the business person can comprehend the terms she's using, rather than hearing the cry for help that's inherent in the question!

Getting into the habit of talking about value in business terms is both smart and useful for any project manager. It can help reduce the number of communication problems you'll have, and smooth the way for the customer and the project team to work more effectively together. After all, if the technical person in the example above had explained that the project was needed so that twice as many customers could use the web site at the same time, all would have been clear to the project manager.

Value equals money. When you're talking about value creation, you'll need to be able to tie the project back to money. Whether the value is direct (that is, you're actually cutting costs or increasing sales), or indirect (you're increasing productivity, helping the organization's public image, and so on), you should at least find it easy to *explain* what the value is. Ideally, it should also be possible to *quantify* that value, for instance, to say "this project will save $30,000, or the equivalent of 50% of a full-time staff member."[3]

You can work out whether a project is worth undertaking in a number of ways. Regardless of which method you use, the most important points to ensure are these:

- The method for calculating value should be crystal clear (use the organization's standard methodology, if one exists).

- Any estimates of time or cost should be provided by the people who are closest to the problem. Only the people who are currently spending two hours a day manually reconciling invoices are going to know exactly how long it takes them.

- The approach you'll use to measure whether the results are actually being achieved should be identified up-front. For example, if you plan to make a saving of two hours per day, exactly how are you going to measure that? By asking the team members? Timing them while they work?

Industry standard methods for calculating the value of a project do exist, but they can be quite complicated and certainly are more involved than those that are commonly used in most organizations. The most important point is to establish that value is being created, so that the organization can be certain to enjoy definite, measurable benefits if the project is undertaken.

When the time comes to measure that benefit in a more sophisticated way, perhaps to justify funding or to compare similar opportunities, understanding more about net present value (NPV), return on investment (ROI), internal rate of return (IRR), and similar methods and measures will be useful. Appendix A lists some locations at which you can find out more about these formal metrics.

---

[3] As an aside, be aware that productivity savings seldom translate into staff actually being made redundant, except in very large-scale projects like mergers or factory relocations. The approach that involves measuring the amount of manual work that's removed is used here to illustrate that the team members will have that much extra time to invest in their day-to-day tasks—time which, otherwise, they wouldn't have had.

Now that you've hopefully seen or constructed a proposal for the project you're about to undertake, and you've formed a better idea of what sort of value it will be creating, it's time to move on to look at who will be affected by, and involved in, the project.

# Who Are All These People?

... and what are they doing on my project?

Even the smallest project can impact a number of people. As the project manager, you're at the centre of an intricate web of people who are bound together by their common interest in the project you're managing. Let's meet the various people who are involved in any project, discuss the roles they play, and explore how you can manage their participation.

## Stakeholders

**Stakeholders** are those people who hold a stake in the project—they're people who care about the project's outcome. "Stakeholders" is really a catch-all term that can be used to describe such disparate groups as senior management, end users of systems, customer representatives, administrators, members of the local community, and union representatives. Anyone who feels that the project might affect them could regard themselves as a stakeholder.

How then do you go about identifying stakeholders? And why would you want to do so in the first place?

It's important to identify your stakeholders so that you can understand their points of view, and get an idea of the pressure they'll try to exert on your project. An architect may not think to worry about the local group of amphibian enthusiasts until they start petitioning the local government to withdraw the permission it granted the architect to build on a particular site that is in fact among the last-remaining habitats of great-crested newts—which the architect has never even heard of before![4]

---

[4] You may think I'm being funny here, but that's a real world example! One of the office buildings on the business park where I work had to be delayed because the site was one of the last remaining habitats of the great-crested newt.

Luckily, most stakeholder groups are more obvious than this, and they're usually very keen to have their voices heard from the outset. The way to start identifying stakeholders is to think about the project itself:

- What are you building?
- What business processes are you changing?
- Who are the people that are currently executing those business processes?
- How will they be impacted by the change?

The easiest stakeholders to identify are those who are directly affected by the project. If we consider this chapter's case study project, in which you're introducing a web site to deal with customer orders, queries, and complaints, we can readily see that the main group affected will be the customer service team. The management of that team will also be affected, as will the IT staff who need to help make the existing call-tracking system integrate with your new web site. And, of course, the actual customers will be affected too—some of them may love the idea of reporting issues via a web site, but others will be concerned that the change in technology will mean slower, less personalized service.

Thinking a little more broadly, we also realize that the sales and marketing teams are stakeholders in the project. After all, as soon as they heard about the possibility of the customer web site, they had the influence to get it prioritized over the other potential projects! After the project proposals were drawn up and you realized that the four projects really needed to be combined to deliver the true business value, the product supply team, who's in charge of the warehouse (and therefore the inventory system), were also identified as stakeholders. Can you think of anyone else who might be affected?

Sometimes the most important stakeholders to worry about are those who are less obviously linked to the project. Senior managers who have promised to deliver a "step change" in the efficiency of the call centre group, or those who are trying to prove that the entire department could be outsourced to Bangalore, may keep their motives closer to their chests. Equally, interest groups from outside the company (whether they're politicians, consumer groups, or the local amphibian enthusiasts' society) may be difficult to locate.

Don't get too hung up on identifying every possible person who might care about your project, but do make the effort to involve those that are obviously interested. Talk to people in the organization about who will be affected and actively seek out those who you believe will care most. Understand their concerns and think about how to involve them in the project. After all, taking the initiative and defining how they will be involved is better than ignoring them, then later having them force their way into a project meeting and explode at everyone!

We'll now look at two special groups of stakeholders—the project board and the project team itself.

## The Project Board

The project board is a small group of people whose main responsibility is to make the really big project decisions. Much as you, as the project manager, have an incredibly important role to play, and indeed will make many of the day-to-day decisions, you'll always be focused on delivering the project. The project board is there to make the really big strategic decisions—even if that means potentially killing the project.

Your project's board should consist of:

- the project sponsor
- a technical advisor
- a business advisor or domain expert (if needed)

The **project sponsor** is the embodiment of the project customer, that is, the person for whom the project is being delivered. Typically, this person will be the head of the department that will benefit the most from the project, though in some cases, if multiple groups within the company will all benefit from the project, the sponsor may be someone who's even higher up within the organization. This person is usually also the one who's paying for the project, so he or she will have a clear interest in ensuring that value for money is delivered. Ultimate decision-making authority resides with the project sponsor.

Choosing the right project sponsor is very important. This person needs to be interested enough to stay involved and take the project seriously. He or she equally needs to be senior enough to have the authority to make the very big decisions—even the decision to cancel the project if necessary.

Sometimes, you don't get to choose the project sponsor: either someone has already been selected, or is chosen without much input from you. This can be fine—the sponsor may be interested in the project and have sufficient authority to help you achieve results. Equally, they may seem disinterested and disengaged from the project.

 **Dealing with Disinterested Sponsors**

If you find yourself working with a disinterested sponsor, sit down with that person and discuss the project, his or her role within it, and your expectations. If the person can be the sponsor you need, engaging him or her in a discussion may well pique the sponsor's interest and lead to more active involvement. Alternatively, if you need more than the sponsor can give, he or she may step aside quietly, or even volunteer to help you find a replacement.

The **technical advisor** and **business advisor** or **domain expert** are there to provide perspective and advice to the project sponsor. The sponsor may not understand the full technical or business process implications of certain decisions that need to be made through the project—he or she can rely on these advisors to promote and encourage the best possible decision.

As project manager, you should expect to meet with the project board regularly to provide progress updates and discuss any key decisions. Usually, the role of the project manager is to lay out the options and recommend the course of action that you believe is the best way forward. However, it's important to realize that the project board's job is to make the really crucial decisions, which may even extend to stopping the project if it's been delayed too long, is too expensive, or if there's evidence that the desired value will not or cannot be delivered.

Usually, the biggest challenge with the project board is not to identify the three members, but to keep the size of the board to just three! All sorts of stakeholders will feel that they should be on the project board, particularly in organizations where decision-making authority is seen to convey status.

What you ideally want is for all stakeholders to feel that they're being represented on the board by at least one of the three members, rather than needing to be on the board themselves. This is another reason why project board members are often senior members of the organization—if the other stakeholders report to them (either directly or indirectly), the board members will also be representing their views.

But let's get back to our example. Before we realized that the four projects really needed to be combined, the project might have had a very different project board, as different teams would have been involved and affected. However, for the combined project, we identify that since the customer service, sales, marketing, IT, and product supply departments are *all* affected, John Vaswani, the Head of Operations (which encompasses all these groups) is the right person to be the project sponsor.

The technical advisor will be Sandra Chan, Head of IT, who can advise on how the solutions being proposed will fit with the existing company systems, and how on-going maintenance and support will be completed. The Head of Customer Service, Adam Garcia, will also participate on the board as the business expert. They will, of course, be advised by their own operational teams, but the point is that the project board will include three key people who can make the big calls!

As soon as she heard about the project board being formed, the Head of Marketing wanted to be included as well. You had a difficult decision to make. As far as possible, it's best to keep the number of board members low. Any efforts to expand the board can easily snowball until half of your stakeholders want to be on the board casting their votes! That said, if the project scope is broad, and you're going to be working on business processes in a wide range of areas, as in this case, it can be useful to have multiple business experts.

In this case, however, you sit down with the marketing chief and explain that the marketing department will still be consulted—you want to have some of the marketing team on the project as "consultants" to ensure that the solution that's developed isn't solely focused internally, on the customer service team's needs. The marketing department's point of view would also be represented on the project board by John Vaswani, who, as Head of Operations, will be interested in making sure that all of the different areas work together as efficiently as possible.

You come away from this meeting with a double win: content with the proposed arrangement, the Head of Marketing has already assigned some of her team members to be more directly involved with your project. You've also managed to keep the size of the project board down to three, which will make the decision-making process much smoother than it would have been if the team was bigger.

## The Project Team

The other stakeholders that are very obviously quite invested in the project's success are the project team members themselves. These are the folks who are working alongside you to deliver the actual work and, as such, they're essential! Depending on your circumstances, the project team members may herald from different backgrounds and companies, and may have been brought together just for this specific project, or they might comprise an existing team that's been charged with focusing its efforts on this new challenge.

Whichever is the case, ensuring that you have the right mix of abilities on the project team is key. We'll talk a lot more in later chapters about how to help your team members work well together, but the first step towards harmony is to make sure that they have the skills necessary for the job.

As with the other stakeholders, you'll want to understand where the people in your project team are coming from. You may well find yourself with a mix of contractors and employees, some working full-time and some part-time. What are their personal motivations? How do they feel about working on this project? Are they viewing it as the opportunity of a lifetime or a punishment? Do they feel they have the needed skills, or are they worried that they're out of their depth?

"Hang on a second!" I hear you protest. "I'm not their manager. Why should I care about how they're feeling?"

Even though you may not be their line manager, or responsible for their careers, you still need to care about how your team members feel, since this will affect your project. People will always be the most complicated component of any project, so it's crucial that you become adept at understanding them. While this may seem daunting, the reality is that just by listening to your team and trying to understand where they're coming from, you'll learn almost everything you need to know. The elements that you don't uncover by talking to them, you'll learn from watching them work together (or failing to work together, as the case may be!).

When you're starting a project with a new team, I suggest that you sit down, one on one, with each individual. Ask them what they're looking forward to and what they're feeling apprehensive about. Share your vision for the project and how you see them being involved. Try not to pile on the expectations too much, though; rather, focus on listening to how they feel about the project and what concerns they might have.

## What If It's Just Me?

Sometimes you may find yourself being both project manager and project team. In this situation you might doubt the need for project management. Your doubts would be valid! If you're a team of one, the tools and practices of project management that focus on team collaboration won't be as useful. With no need to share and communicate, you can keep track of your tasks and deliverables however you like.

Realistically though, much of the true value of project management is in communicating to the stakeholders and project board, rather than your team. Project success depends on the involvement, trust and often contributions of the stakeholders. Equipping the project board to make well-informed key decisions is also extremely important.

If you are a freelancer or similar, primarily working solo on projects, then you may well want to strip down to just the essential tools and best practices. By focusing on the tools that smooth your interfaces to stakeholders and project board, you will get the most out of your investment in project management. For more information, see Appendix A.

# Stakeholder Tools and Best Practices

Let's examine some of the tools and best practices that will help you identify stakeholders and manage their involvement in your project.

## The Project Organization Chart

A **project organization chart** is a simple graphical illustration of who's involved in the project and where they fit in the overall organizational, or project, plan. First you'd include yourself, the project manager, with the project team linked in beneath. You report to the project board, which is led by the project sponsor. Depending on the specifics of your project, you will likely then group the remaining stakeholders into their respective areas (for instance, end users and IT staff). These groups are shown on either side of the project team, since they'll be giving input as the project progresses, as Figure 2.1 reflects.

To create a project organization chart, follow these steps:

- Write down the names of *everyone* who's involved in the project.

- Group them according to their roles—project board members, stakeholders, and project team members. In most cases, you'll need to split the stakeholders' group further into the various stakeholder categories.

- Chart the results graphically, with project board at the top, the project team in the middle, and stakeholders radiating out from them. If some of the stakeholders report to the project board members, it may be worth indicating this on the chart.

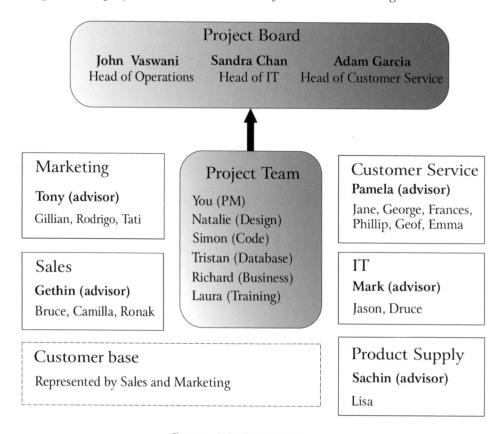

Figure 2.1. A simple organization chart

The project organization chart is useful because it illustrates to everyone within the organization who's directly involved in the project (that is, the project team and board), and who has a more advisory role to play. You may need to consider establishing a team of key stakeholders who will be directly involved in the project, whether they're providing realistic testing for the product, or helping with the requirements gathering task.

 **Is There Anybody Out There?**

If people in your project haven't worked together in the past, or if they're spread across offices or even time zones, it may be worth adding their photos and contact information to the organizational chart. Making it easy for team members and stakeholders to get in touch with each other can only aid communication and collaboration.

As your project progresses, keeping the project organization chart up to date becomes more and more important. Projects tend to get more complex as they continue, and more people get involved, and understanding where any given person fits into the bigger picture is important if you are to have a context for his or her input. A particular stakeholder who complains about everything, wants to be involved in every decision, and generally makes a nuisance of himself or herself can be difficult to deal with. But, by looking at the project organization chart, you might realize that that particular individual is really a minor stakeholder, but reports to the project sponsor. In the process, you may also recognize that the person is trying to get noticed in the run-up to the annual review period, which can help you work out how best to deal with this individual.

Perhaps you'll choose to have a word with that person in private, and ask for his or her help in making the project a success; you may also involve this person more obviously in the project so he or she obtains the desired visibility. On the other hand, if the person is being positively destructive, you might choose to have a word with the sponsor to see if that individual's efforts couldn't be redirected somewhere more constructive.

### Organizational Chart Evolution

Quite often, your organizational chart will evolve. Before your project has really started, you might not have a full picture of what the team will look like, and which stakeholders will be involved. It's a useful tool from the very start, though, so always start by drawing a rough chart on a piece of paper, even if you only progress to a shareable electronic version later on during the project's Initiating or Planning phases.

## The Communication Plan

A communication plan is a simple document that outlines how you will communicate the project process, how frequently you'll do so, who will be invited or involved, and who will be in charge of making sure the communication occurs.

The communication plan should cover everything from monthly email updates (which might be sent to all the interested parties) to daily meetings (for the project team) and fortnightly board meetings (organized by you with the project board). It might also define what specific information you'll be reporting to a much wider public—for instance, for particularly important projects, it might be worth posting summary updates on the homepage of the company's intranet. Therefore, anyone who's interested in the project, or feels that their own work might somehow overlap with what your team is doing, can see what's going on. You should *always* include your contact details alongside this type of communication—after all, you never know who might warn you of the next big project hiccup!

### Letting Them Know

Believe it or not, some of the value of your communication plan lies just in letting people know they'll be kept informed! Uncertainty is the cause of a lot of noise in projects. The communication plan can not only reassure stakeholders that they'll be kept in the loop, but can also inform them of how and when this will happen. It can also help you to ensure their input is directed to the appropriate people and points in the project, and avoid having them crash your team meetings!

# Initiating Your Project

Now we're ready to really get going with the project! So let's look at why initiating your project well is so important, and how you should go about it. We'll also investigate some of the tools and best practices for doing so.

## The Purpose of Initiating

The purpose of the Initiating phase is to set the project up for success. I often argue that it is the most important phase of the project life cycle, since, if it's neglected, the results can be catastrophic. After all, the beginning of the project is the point at which you form with the customer the contract (both formal and informal) that explains what will be delivered, roughly how it will be done, and when it will be ready.

The formal contract will be the piece of paper you sign, but the informal contract is the unspoken understanding between yourself and the other interested parties. Often the informal contract is the more important of the two—people are more interested in what they believe you're going to deliver than the specifics written in the contract. This is especially true if the contracts are drawn up by a lawyer or separate part of the organization. If you're working internally and there's no formal contract, the informal contract is all that matters!

### Keeping the Project in Perspective

Unless this is agreed on, you and the customers can walk away with completely different understandings of what you're trying to accomplish. These differences of perspective will only creep out of the woodwork to cause you trouble later on, unless you consciously shine a light on them during the project's initiation.

Initiating is also the best chance you'll get to define success. At the very outset you can agree on the project's success criteria—key elements that need to be delivered for the project to be successful. These criteria will then help guide you throughout the project. Of course, if it's obvious from your initial discussions that the success criteria aren't clearly linked to the business purpose of the project, again, you've uncovered a potential stumbling block very early, before too much energy has been invested in the project.

# The Process of Initiating

The process of project initiation is quite simple. Gather information about:

- why the project is happening
- what needs to be delivered and how this will be done
- who will be involved
- the timings to which the project will be delivered

Make sure to get input from all the key stakeholders:

- Summarize the why, what, how, who, and when of the project into a Project Initiation Document.

- Review the Project Initiation Document with the project board and key stakeholders to get their agreement.

- Hold a kickoff meeting to herald the start of the project, share the success criteria, and plan going forward with the project team, board members, and key stakeholders.

There may well be a number of unfamiliar terms in that process explanation, but don't worry about that just now. We're about to look at the different tools and best practices that will help you get your project off to a flying start. The key point to take away from the initiating process is that you should start the project with everyone on the same page, and move forward towards a common, agreed goal.

# Initiation Tools and Best Practices

The project's Initiation phase will be eased by the following key tools and practices.

## The Project Initiation Document

The **Project Initiation Document** (PID) summarizes the what, how, when, and why of the project. It represents the agreement between all parties on what the project is about and, importantly, why the project is being undertaken. Although obviously some facets will change during the course of the project (notably the details of how the project is achieved, the project's timings, and the resources available) the fundamentals of what the project is and why it'll make a difference to the organization should be pretty stable.

The Project Initiation Document needs to summarize:

- the project's objective (what you're trying to achieve)
- the key deliverables (how you're going to achieve the objective)
- the overall rationale for the project (why you're undertaking it)
- the initial timings (when it will be achieved)
- the project's initial organization (who is involved)

Other elements that should be included in the initiation document are key assumptions and constraints, and success criteria. You may also want to include high-level information about the risk and quality management approaches you'll use, although this detail is often included in the project plan, rather than the PID.

It's important that the PID be as concise as possible. The shorter the PID, the greater are the chances that the stakeholders will actually read it at the outset, which can smooth the project's progress over time.

Once you've written your initiation document, don't just stick it on a shelf and forget about it! The document should be agreed upon up-front with your project's key stakeholders (including the project sponsor and board), and should be referred to subsequently throughout the project. Whenever you're making difficult decisions about which changes to the project's scope or design should be accepted, referring to the project's original objectives and success criteria will prove invaluable.

### A PID Is Not a Contract!

The Project Initiation Document is *not* a legal contract. For a start, it's much shorter than any contract I've ever seen! The PID can't replace the contract, either. If you're a freelancer or a business providing services to a client, you still need to make sure that you have all your regular contracts in place. You probably want to refer to the PID in the contract, but since it's accepted that the actual execution of the project will likely diverge from the descriptions in the PID, you can't rely on it as you would a contract.

If you're employed by an organization, and providing project management services to another part of the same company, it will depend very much on the company culture whether or not you need to have a contract in place. Many companies don't have formal contracts for internal projects. In such cases, the PID serves an even more important role, since it's the only place where the expectations that the project team and customer have of each other are recorded.

Let's consider the project initiation document for our example project, which will address all four opportunities originally identified during the discovery phase.

The first section defines the business need—it's simply a paragraph or two that describes the opportunity for the project, as Figure 2.2 shows.

## PROJECT INITIATION DOCUMENT
### Customer Service Modernization Project

**BUSINESS NEED** *(WHY)*

Currently, the customer service division does a lot of manual work. Each person in the CS team spends more than a day a week dealing with paperwork, when the primary focus should be customer interaction. Tracking orders, queries and complaints is difficult and again a lot of time is spent manually pulling together information so that reporting can be done. When answering a call, the customer service agent is not able to see all of the recent orders, queries and complaints for the given customer, so customers often have to repeat information depending on who they get to speak to.

In addition, there is no linkage with the inventory systems, so each day a number of calls have to be fielded by the product supply team just so that those taking orders can check that there are sufficient stocks to fulfill the order before placing it. Customers have also fed back via the sales teams and their customer service contacts that they would like to be able to place orders and log queries and complaints online or via email, rather than having to call up each time.

Figure 2.2. The Business Need section of the PID

Then comes the project objective, as shown in Figure 2.3. You'll notice that this part is written to a particular format that includes:

- an overall description of what the project's about
- a description of the key areas to be addressed
- a definition of the specific business benefit that the project will realize

This is a very useful format for describing objectives. You may find another standard in use in your organization, though, and it's often best to use the format that people are familiar and comfortable with.

---

**PROJECT OBJECTIVE** *(WHAT)*

TO: Modernize the customer service processes and systems

IN A WAY THAT:
- Removes manual rework from the processes and procedures
- Effectively connects ordering, inventory and customer query systems
- Provides appropriate reporting and tracking of customer orders, queries and complaints
- Allows customers to interact via telephone, email or web phone, both to make initial contact and to check for updates

SO THAT:
Customer satisfaction is increased to a score of 60% and running costs decreased by $20,000 per annum.

---

Figure 2.3. The Project Objective section of the PID

 **SMAC Your Objectives**

Your objectives should be **SMAC**: specific, measurable, actionable, and consistent. The key feature is that at the end of the project, you should be able to say "yes, we did that" or "no, we failed." There should be no gray areas. Throughout the project, you should be able to track the team's progress towards those objectives.

The next section of the PID identifies the project deliverables, as shown in Figure 2.4; it describes how you're going to achieve the objective. This description must necessarily be completed on a very high level, because the project is just getting started—you haven't done any detailed planning yet. Here, you just need to give an idea of the biggest chunks of work to be done. Try to make sure that no deliverable will take longer than a month to complete, though—if you're still looking at phases of three months or more, break those phases into a little more detail.

---

**PROJECT DELIVERABLES** *(HOW)*
- Evaluation and recommendation as to whether to implement a generic CRM solution or whether to build one internally
- Analysis of existing customer service processes and procedures and recommendation for improvements
- Implementation of CRM solution in line with new processes and requirements
- Interfaces to new CRM system from inventory and other existing systems
- Customer-facing web site and email address, for logging orders, queries and complaints, as well as for status updates

---

Figure 2.4. The Project Deliverables section of the PID

Next, we come to the project timeline. If the project is one that you're familiar with, you might already have a good idea of rough timelines for the various phases as well as the project overall. If you can, list the major deliverables against the week or month in which they'll be delivered (there's no fine detail here, of course—you'd really only use a weekly breakdown if the project time was less than three months). In this case, the first two pieces of work are going to define the rest of the timeline, so we're only setting a deadline for these two phases, as Figure 2.5 shows.

---

**ESTIMATED TIMELINE** *(WHEN)*

Since there is significant investigatory and analysis work to be done, there is a great deal of uncertainty in terms of how long this project will take. The recommendation is to set a deadline for the first two deliverables (identifying whether to buy or build a CRM solution and analyzing and recommending changes to the processes and procedures of the customer service department) of March 1ˢᵗ (2 months from now). At this point, a plan for further work will be presented for project board review.

---

Figure 2.5. The Estimated Timeline section of the PID

## Is it Feasible?

In some organizations, the initial analysis of the business processes and investigation of whether to buy or build a system might form what's known as a **feasibility study** or **feasibility project**. Rather than starting the full project with such uncertainty, a separate smaller project would be undertaken just to work out whether the main project is worth undertaking, and what would be required if it was.

The last part of the PID outlines the project organization. For this project, we've just pasted in the organization chart that we'd already prepared, as in Figure 2.6. Depending on how much the organization values role descriptions, you might want to put in more detail about what's expected of each individual.

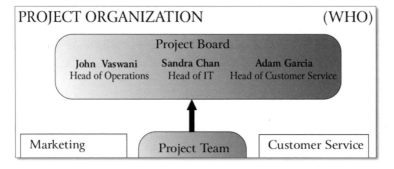

Figure 2.6. The Project Organization section of the PID

Brief details of assumptions and constraints are often included in the Project Initiation Document. If the feasibility study had been split into a separate project, we would have listed all the assumptions we were making about buying the technical solution as compared to building one. However, since this project is starting with an investigation, these sections are not as important as they might be if we were going straight into the Executing phase.

## The Kickoff Meeting

The kickoff meeting is more of a best practice than a tool. It's essentially a meeting at which you bring together the key players in the project to officially get the project started. Usually this will take at least a couple of hours, but you should judge an appropriate timeframe based on the complexity of your project.

The key attendees of the kickoff meeting are the project team and the interested stakeholders. The kickoff meeting is probably the first time that everyone involved will have come together for the project, so it's a great opportunity to get everyone enthused. Since you are (I hope!) working on a project that's important to the future of the organization, you might want to ask the sponsor to say a few words about why he or she thinks the project is important, and what will be achieved, before going into the main discussion points. A typical kickoff meeting agenda might look like this:

- welcome and introduction
- highlights from PID (with a particular focus on the "why" of the project)
- project approach (sharing some of the details of how the project will be managed)
- communication plan (so that everyone knows when they'll hear more)
- plan for moving forward (that is, what will happen in the immediate future)

The fifth point is the one likely to inspire the most debate. Hopefully, through the process of creating the project initiation document (PID), you've ensured that you've captured everyone's opinions about why the project should happen. Conversely, the project approach and communications plan are unlikely to be particularly controversial. But the plan for actually going and tackling the work can inspire rigorous debate!

This is why it's particularly important to have the key stakeholders in the meeting, as well as the team—it would be a rare project on which you won't need their help and input during the actual project activities, so involving them in some of the initial planning work is a smart move.

 **Hand Out the PID**

The real focus of the kickoff meeting is to get everyone aligned on the initiation of the project, so why not hand out a copy of the Project Initiation Document to every attendee? This will make sure everyone has the same information from which to form expectations of what the project will involve, and how it will work.

# Seven Essential Steps for a Successful Initiation

Follow this advice, and you'll drastically increase your chances of running a successful project that makes a real difference!

1. Pick projects that are important to the organization and to its future.

2. Make sure that you have appropriate resources for your project—whether those include people, equipment, or budget.

3. Include the people who are affected by, and interested in, your project in the project itself—their inputs and opinions matter!

4. Set up a project board with the necessary members right at the beginning of the project, not just when the difficult decisions need to be made.

5. Create a Project Initiation Document and review it with the project team, board members, and key stakeholders.

6. Get your project started with a kickoff meeting, both to ensure the alignment of stakeholder expectations, and get everyone enthusiastic about the project!

7. Create a communications plan that outlines who needs to be kept informed about your project's progress, and how you're going to communicate with those people.

# Summary

In this chapter, we firstly looked at the discovery phase—how projects are identified and prioritized based on the business value they can deliver, and their relative importance to the future of the organization as a whole. We then considered a discovery tool and a best practice: project proposals and value creation, respectively. The former is a short summary of the project, which can be compared to other project proposals in order to evaluate its priority. Value creation is an important task because unless you know up-front what business benefits you are trying to deliver, you won't know whether or not the project has been successful when you complete it!

Next, we looked at all the people involved in the project, ranging from stakeholders (essentially anyone who's affected by the project) to the project board (which makes the really big decisions) and the project team (those that actually undertake the work). The key tools we discussed included the project organization chart and communication plan.

Finally—and most importantly—we looked at actually getting your project off the ground! The key tools we considered were the PID and kickoff meeting. The Project Initiation Document (PID) summarizes the what, why, how, who, and when of the project, so that you can share and agree on these details with the project's stakeholders. The kickoff meeting brings everyone involved together to start the project, helping the stakeholders feel engaged in the project, and demonstrating the commitment of the project board.

 **Create a PID for an Existing Project**

Make sure that you familiarize yourself with the tools that we've been talking about. One really good way of coming to terms with these tools is to retrospectively create some of the documents for a project you're currently working on (or one that you've already completed). A great way to start is by creating a project proposal and a PID.

# Chapter 3

# Getting The Job Done

At this point you hopefully understand what your project is and more importantly why you're doing it. So what next? We're going to look at the next three phases of the project life cycle that we discussed in Chapter 1: Planning, Executing, and Controlling. These phases form a loop, which we go through repeatedly until the project closes.

## Planning

Planning is arguably the most important phase of your project. Skimp here and you'll suffer later. But if you invest in planning, the entire project will run much more smoothly.

In this section, we'll first look at why you need to plan. We'll discuss what aspects you should plan, and we'll see how to go about creating an initial project plan. Finally, we'll investigate the different tools and techniques that will help you become a master planner!

# Why Plan?

If you've ever worked on a project for which the project plan seemed to be miles long and permanently out of date, you're probably skeptical about project plans. I don't blame you! It's perfectly understandable to think planning is a waste of time if it never seems to do any good.

That said, there are a number of good reasons to plan:

- to understand your project better

- to work out the best way to approach things

- to communicate to both your team and the client or customer exactly how the project is going to be approached

- to help you get work done and keep track of progress

- to provide direction

Sometimes, planning is just as much about the process as the eventual end result. Planning can be useful simply because it allows you to allocate time to really thinking about how the project will be achieved. This process will help you understand your project better, as you'll have outlined the biggest chunks of work, you'll understand what needs to be delivered, and you'll have noted any key dependencies at play in the project (that is, things that have to be completed before other things can be started).

Likewise, a better understanding of what the project will entail can help you identify the best approach to tackling it. Are you going to be able to give good estimates because you've done similar projects in the past, or is this project a whole new world of unknown complexity?

Plans are often most valuable as a shared understanding of how the project is going to be approached. Once you move on from tiny projects for which you and your laptop are the only resources required, you'll realize how valuable plans can be. You'll start to have more people involved—clients or customers, the project team, and a project board. These people will be asked to make key decisions, and they'll want to understand the impacts of those decisions. One really powerful way to illustrate this is to show them how different choices will affect the project plan and schedule.

Without a plan, it becomes very hard to execute and control your project. How do you know what to do next, or whether you're on track? Of course, this doesn't mean that the plan should be full of minute detail—it isn't a replacement for your personal to-do list. Nor should you spend more time updating the percentage complete figures on the plan than doing actual work. Striking the right balance is the key to successful planning, so we'll look at it in detail in the coming sections.

Planning was once explained to me as being similar to driving a long distance. The plan you need for a journey doesn't include every minor course correction, and it can't accommodate your need to overtake a black SUV 39 minutes into the journey. Instead, the focus is on providing the direction and identifying the key decision points (when to get on the freeway, which way to turn at the traffic lights, and so on) that you'll need to work through to get to your destination.

## What to Plan

Traditional project planning is focused around tasks—jobs that you need to do, or actions you need to take. At first glance, this might seem sensible. A task-based plan will literally give you a list of items that you need to do, like a to-do list for the entire project.

The problem with tasks, however, is that they're hard to measure, and are rarely a good indication of progress. If you've completed 80% of your tasks, does that mean that 80% of the project is complete? How can you measure whether a task is 10% complete or 90% complete? This problem is particularly common in knowledge work, where the intricacies of developing an algorithm, or designing the right layout, can take much more (or occasionally much less) time than expected.

So, if we're not planning tasks, what should we plan instead?

We should plan **deliverables**—the actual end-products of your project, be they tangible (machines, buildings, cash) or intangible (software, a brand identity, and so on).

The difference between a **task** and a deliverable is that the task is the job you're busy doing (building, designing, creating), while the deliverable is the product you end up with (a wall, a design, a document). For instance, the task might be "lay the foundations," but the end product or deliverable is the foundations themselves.

With some tasks, it can difficult to identify the associated deliverables, but you should always focus on the end product, rather than the task itself. For instance, in a software project, the team might spend a lot of time on the task of writing documentation or detailing designs, but what really matters at the end of the day is the documentation or design itself.

### The Perils of Percent Complete

Measuring the percentage of tasks complete (or similar techniques) is an extremely dangerous practice. The biggest problem is that it's a very subjective measure—you're usually relying on individuals to define whether they're 10% complete or 90% complete.

Why is this a problem?

**People are overoptimistic.**
How often have you thought something would take half the amount time that it actually took?

**People lie.**
They know when you want the job done and will reassure you that it'll be ready, even if they haven't actually started (often this comes after the overoptimism mentioned above).

**Work expands to fill the available time.**
Even if a task seems to be half-done after two days, if you've allocated six days to it, there's a good chance that it will take six days to achieve.

As a general rule, measures that involve just two possibilities (that is, is it finished, or is it not finished?) are much more effective and accurate. This is another compelling reason to focus on deliverables rather than tasks—deliverables are either complete or incomplete.

## How to Plan

Planning a project for the first time is a six-step process:

1. Break down the project into pieces small enough to work with.

2. Identify dependencies.

3. Estimate how long each piece will take.

4. Add some contingency.

5. Consider the risks.

6. Represent the plan in a format that the team, board, and stakeholders will understand and follow.

Let's look at this process in detail.

## Breaking Down the Deliverables

The first task you need to work out is how you're going to break the single end-goal of your project into individual deliverables that are small enough to be both achievable and measurable. Striking the right balance here is crucial: deliverables that are too large can be paralyzing (they're so big you don't even know where to start!), but if you focus too much on the detail, you'll be micro-managing the project.

Let's look at an example. Suppose we're developing a web site for a local cake shop—one that's never had any kind of online presence before. Although the business has sound reasons for approaching the project (the owners believe a web site will give them a broader reach and will thereby increase sales), they're a little hazy on exactly what it is they want. This is where you come in. You've had some discussions with the owner and the staff, trying to get a basic list of requirements together and to generate some ideas. Now you're at the point of trying to pull together what you think should be built into a project plan.

An initial attempt to break down the project into realizable deliverables gave us the list shown in Figure 3.1.

---

**Cake Shop Web Site**
- "About the store" section (including contact details/how to find us)
- "Order online" section
    - Online catalog
    - Admin interface (for adding, editing, deleting products)
    - Shopping basket functionality
        - Add an item
        - Edit the basket (add, edit, delete)
        - Payments
        - Confirmation emails
        - Interface to orders/delivery system
- "Get a quote" contact form for custom cakes for special occasions
- "Special occasions gallery" to show off past custom work
    - Slideshow functionality
    - Photo upload
- Web hosting and domain name registration
- Email address setup

---

Figure 3.1. Initial deliverables breakdown

For this example, we're assuming that you've already agreed whether you are building the site from scratch or whether a particular set of technologies will be used—if not, then investigating, recommending, and agreeing on the technology choices would need to be added to the plan as well.

The chunks of work listed in Figure 3.1 represent the main deliverables, and have been broken down further when they seemed too big. At this initial stage, we're not trying to get into a great deal of detail—we're just aiming to break everything down into chunks that will take less than a week to complete each. In other words, the lowest level of detail for tasks in a given project should constitute no more than five days' work.

# Identifying Dependencies

The next step is to identify the **dependencies**—which deliverables depend on other deliverables. For instance, if the Get a Quote form was going to send an email direct to the head baker, the relevant email addresses would need to be set up first.

It's important, however, to focus on the *true* dependencies. Since many of us start out doing projects in which we simultaneously project manage *and* do all the work, it's easy to get into the mentality of believing that all work has to happen sequentially. When you're on your own, you're typically only able to work on one item at a time, so you work on one task after the other. This is what in project management-speak is known as a **resource dependency**: the only reason why the two deliverables can't be worked on in parallel is because you have a limited number of people (or resources) available to do the work.

You may well end up putting some tasks in sequence because of resource restrictions, but leave that until later. For now, try to focus on the work that *by its nature* demands to be done in sequence. You may find that there aren't many tasks that are truly dependent on each other. This is quite typical in knowledge work, whereas traditional project management areas, such as construction, are awash with dependencies—foundations need to be dug, and concrete poured and set, before a structure can be built, for example.

Dependency identification can help you recognize holes in your initial breakdown of deliverables. It's only when we look at the dependencies for each section that we realize that we haven't actually got the site design in the plan! All the sections of the web site that we're planning to build depend on some agreement on an overall design, but at the moment, this is implicit in the plan. We need to flag that this needs to be done, and the overall design scheme must be agreed on, before any of the individual deliverables can be completed.

Identifying dependencies can be as simple as drawing some arrows on your list of deliverables to indicate which items precede others. If your list of deliverables starts to look more like a piece of abstract modern art than a plan at this point, you might want to consider moving it over into a flowchart, as I've done in Figure 3.2.

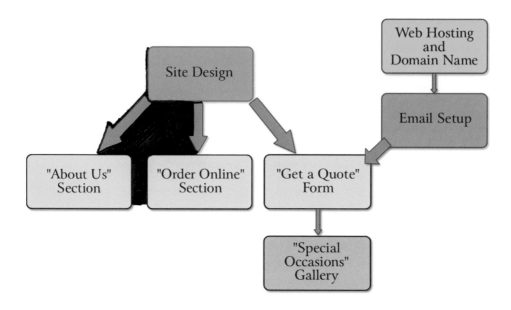

Figure 3.2. A simple dependency flowchart for our plan

## Estimating Time

Estimating the time a project will take is probably the most maligned (and most frequently overlooked) part of the planning process. When they're pressed for time, many project managers make the mistake of creating estimates themselves by plucking numbers out of the air seemingly at random (or so it feels to the team when they're presented with the time frames in which they must achieve everything!).

The point of **estimating** is to predict how long the production of the various deliverables will take, so that you can build an initial project schedule. Although schedules are often mistaken for project plans, in fact a schedule is just one *part* of a project plan. We'll discuss this more a little later, when we talk about representing your plan.

The key rule to remember when estimating time is this:

*The person who will actually undertake a given piece of work should create the estimates.*

It's as simple as that.

If you're trying to estimate for work that will be performed by more than one person, that subteam needs to agree on an estimate together. Ideally, you'll already have involved your team in the breaking down of the work into logical chunks *and* in working out the dependencies, but even if you've gone it alone on those parts of the process, it's absolutely essential to involve them in the estimating process.

Why is this so important? Because estimates need to be realistic. More than that, estimates need to be realistic for the people who'll work with them. How would you feel if someone came along and told you that the work you're going to do is going to take you one week? If your project manager is lucky, then he's magically guessed an achievable estimate. If he's as unlucky as you feel right now, he's got it totally wrong. The end result? You're unhappy because you're having unrealistic deadlines forced on you, and he's going to be unhappy because you're never going to get that work delivered in a week.

Okay, so you've got the point that the right people need to be involved in this task. But how does this estimating process actually work?

If you're extraordinarily lucky, you'll be part of an experienced team that's working on a project that's very similar to all the other projects the team members have ever done. It's like being blessed with a great builder: they can predict fairly accurately how long it'll take for them to build a wall, or lay flooring in your kitchen, because they've done it umpteen times before. If you're in this situation, then thank your lucky stars and listen carefully to the estimates your team members are giving you.

More likely, at least some aspects of the project will be new. Perhaps some of the folks in your team have never worked on this kind of project before; perhaps a new technology or approach is being employed. Whatever the specifics, there's likely to be some element that casts uncertainty into the ring. In such cases, you want to look at two aspects. The first is to consider breaking down the deliverables further—by looking at smaller parts of the job, the person creating the estimation may be able to be more accurate, or to draw more parallels to past experience. The second is to make use of some averaging techniques.

A few averaging techniques are available, and you can choose the one you prefer. The options vary in complexity, but two of the simpler equations are:

■ *(Most optimistic + least optimistic) ÷ 2*

This really is just the average of your longest and shortest estimates.

■ *[Most optimistic + (4 x most likely) + least optimistic] ÷ 6*

The point of this method is to give extra weight to the most likely estimate.

Probably a more important task, once you've obtained your estimates, is to work out how you feel about them. Your own feelings about the reliability of your estimates will determine how you communicate them.

One common—and serious—problem with estimating is that people involved in the project often mistake estimates for something else entirely. Some mistake them for guesses that have no credibility. These people are likely to steamroll over your project plan because they believe that all the estimates have just been pulled out of thin air. Others mistake estimates for targets or deadlines—they will then hold you to those initial estimates, lambasting you if you don't "meet your targets."

Both of these misconceptions are dangerous because they force you and your team to react defensively. If people outside the project team see your estimates as guesstimates, the team will start to do this as well—after all, why should they put proper effort into the estimating task if that effort isn't rewarded? Equally, if estimates are seen as targets, the smart thing for individuals to do is to give themselves more time than they really need, so that they can guarantee to meet these targets.

In fact, it's very difficult to create accurate estimates for work that will be performed more than six to eight weeks from now. When you're working on a particular phase of the project, you can plan that phase with reasonable accuracy, getting right down into the detail of what needs to be achieved. But the phase that starts three months from now? Forget it. It's either so far away you don't have an opinion, or it has that rosy tint that smacks of overoptimism.

Instead of planning the entire project in one fell swoop, you should use a **rolling wave** approach that gives very rough, broad-based estimates for any deliverable that's too far out to estimate (typically more than eight weeks away), and only putting the effort in to breaking down the detail, and estimating properly, the work that's coming in the immediate future.

By communicating that this is the approach you'll use, you'll also help to combat the two side effects listed above—you can openly admit that the estimates for the second and third phases of the project are rough as sandpaper, but defend the accuracy of the estimates for the work coming in the next few weeks. This way, your team members can be confident that they're investing time and energy in making estimates that'll be protected, and those who want to steamroll your project schedule will be forced to restrict their activities to the later phases of the project. And by the time you *get* to those later phases in the project, you'll have data to defend the accuracy of your estimates for the first phase, and to knock back any criticism of your methods.

 **Estimating Conventions**

A method for estimating that's championed by Kevin Lawver is initially to use t-shirt sizes (XXL, XL, L, M, S, XS) to designate the rough size of a deliverable or task. Then, as the rolling wave approaches, proper estimates should be represented in hours. The difference in measurement highlights the firmness of the estimate—any deliverable marked as L is obviously less accurate than the estimate—say, 17 hours—for a specific deliverable.

## Adding Contingency

In theory, now that you've finished estimating, you should have a fairly good idea of how long it's going to take to deliver the project. You also have more detail about when the project's initial deliverables will be produced. Now it's time to add contingency.

**Contingency** is extra time that's allowed in the schedule to cover unexpected events, such as a milestone that takes longer to achieve than you planned, a problem that's harder to solve than you realized, or local transport links being severed due to a collapsed mine shaft, which puts the entire team back a day—or longer.[1]

---

[1] This might sound silly, but it actually happened at my office recently. The city I live in is connected by a tram network. A forgotten mineshaft collapsing directly underneath one of the main lines meant that everyone who relied on public transport to get to work (a significant percentage of the workforce!) had their commuting time doubled for a few weeks whilst the city worked to restore the tram services.

As well as catering to the unexpected, contingency is a good way to factor in *expected* events that'll have an impact on the schedule. These events include task switching, other work, and personal commitments.

When you're breaking deliverables into milestones, and estimating how long it will take to deliver them, it's normal to assume that everyone's working a full week. When someone asks us how long something will take, we naturally assume that they mean "if you were focusing on this and this alone, how long would it take?" The reality, though, is that we're seldom focused on just one thing.

Most people are working on more than one item at a time. Some efficiency is therefore lost due to **task switching**—the time it takes to shift from one job to another. As well as task switching, you'll need to take into account all the day-to-day tasks that need taking care of (checking email, answering the phone, and so on), regular events (like departmental meetings, training courses, fire drills), and other events that, though they're less regular, still aren't really helping your project to move forward (organizing the office party, taking time off for a dentist's appointment, and so on).

We also need to think about public holidays, long weekends, illness, the likelihood that team members might be on holiday (which you can keep track of reasonably easily) and that people outside of the team, but on whom you depend, might be away on holiday or on training. The week-long absence of the key infrastructure team member who you need to set up your database links can really throw you off schedule.

So, how do we go about adding contingency to the schedule?

The traditional method has always been to estimate tasks, factor in dependencies, and identify where you have **inherent contingency**. Inherent contingency arises when you have one task that relies on another, and unavoidable time in between the two. So, if Task A is estimated to start on day 10 and to last for three days (until day 13), but Task B cannot start until day 16, in effect, you can take six days to complete Task A before it will start to affect the project. In addition to these cases of inherent contingency, you'll probably also deliberately add contingency to risky tasks. This could either be achieved by increasing the estimates for those tasks, or by specifically adding extra contingency into your schedule. Some practitioners suggest automatically adding 40% to any estimate to combat overoptimistic tendencies and to allow time for things to go wrong.

As I explained earlier, however, planning tasks (and then measuring the percentage complete) is a dangerous approach. Instead, we intend to plan deliverables and milestones, focusing on what we're actually trying to *achieve*, rather than on the actions we'll take to do so. The net effect is that at any given point you can ask "is this deliverable finished?" and there are only two possible answers: yes or no. Given this approach, how do we go about handling contingency?

 **Communicating Contingency to Stakeholders**

Like estimates, contingency is another concept that's often misunderstood by project stakeholders. They want predictability—to know that there's a plan and that it will be followed exactly. Often, this need is exacerbated by the customers of our projects being used to very different styles of work than we are. People who typically work on projects understand that since they're one-off efforts, the time needed to complete a specific milestone can vary. By contrast, many of our customers are the people in charge of day-to-day operations—they're used to work that's always the same, is completed over and over again, and therefore, is much more predictable in terms of time, cost, quality, and scope.

For this reason, it's also important to think about how to communicate contingency. Depending on the organizational environment in which you find yourself, you might not want to communicate about the existence of contingency at all. I've known plenty of project managers who, realizing that any contingency that the project board saw on the project plan was likely to be forcibly removed ("You don't really need all this *free time* do you?"), chose instead to swallow up all the contingency in the milestones, separately briefing the team on the real estimates and contingency available. Depending on the organization you're working for or with, having your plans rewritten by senior management may be a serious risk.

Maintaining separate plans for management and the project team is just the sort of project management overhead you don't need. Instead, consider what other name you could give to the contingency to make it seem less like free time to your stakeholders, and more like an essential part of the plan. For instance, if you were working on a software development project, it would be perfectly reasonable to have a bug-fixing stage built in to every phase of the project.

We could choose to add contingency to every milestone and deliverable, giving an extra day here and there to every small achievement on our list. In my experience, however, this kind of contingency gets used up on almost every project—as I mentioned above, people tend to work to deliver a piece of work when it's due, allowing the work to expand to fill the available time, rather than trying to meet the original deadline and preserve the contingency. Really, this is just human nature, so allocating contingency at this level of detail encourages contingency to be used up when it isn't really needed.

Instead of adding contingency at this detailed level, then, it's best to add it at a much higher level. Rather than adding a day here, and two days there, add a week of contingency for the entire first release that you're planning. How much contingency will you add? The way to answer this question is to imagine that everything possible goes wrong over that phase of the project—how much time would you like to have up your sleeve to recover? How much time would mean the difference between the project's failure and its success?

## Considering the Risks

Risk management is considered as part of the planning process because panic rarely results in the best approach for dealing with an issue. Risks are no more than elements that might go wrong in your project—they could be internal ("We're using the latest version of SharePoint server and the learning curve might mean it take longer than expected.") or external to your project ("Everyone keeps talking about cost savings and restructuring—does that mean I'm going to lose half my team midproject?").

The process for creating a Risk Management Plan is as follows:

1. Identify potential risks.
2. Rate them by likelihood and severity.
3. Choose which risks to plan for.
4. Make plans for dealing with those risks.

The process you use to complete the initial identification step is entirely up to you. Brainstorming with the team, considering issues that have cropped up in previous projects, or even using the "common risks" checklists that exist for your particular industry, are all valid approaches. The main thing is to write down every risk you can think of—there's no need to filter the options at this initial stage.

You then need to rate each risk, first on the likelihood of its occurrence (how likely is it to actually happen?) and then on its severity (how bad is it if this does happen?). Simplicity is king here—use a five-point scale, or even just a high-medium-low selection, to rate the risks on your list.

As an example, let's think back to the cake shop web site building project that we considered earlier. Here are a couple of example risks that we might face on that project shown in Table 3.1:

1. Insufficient photos and content are available for the site.

2. The customer is very busy and doesn't find time to participate in design reviews.

## Table 3.1. Risk Rating

| Risk | Likelihood | Severity | Overall |
| --- | --- | --- | --- |
| Insufficient photos and content | 3 | 4 | 12 |
| Client doesn't participate in design reviews | 3 | 3 | 9 |

The first risk is pretty severe—you won't be able to deliver the project deliverables without pictures and content. I'd score it as a risk of rating four. The likelihood assessment is more subjective. In this case, we've gathered from our discussions with the clients that they're really quite new to the online world, so this risk is not unlikely. We score it a three. To get the total risk figure, we multiply the two numbers together to get 12.

The second risk is less severe—you can probably deliver the site even without full involvement from the customer, but it might not be to your usual standard of quality. I'd rank this risk a three. The customer also seems fairly committed to the project, so we can rank the likelihood of this risk occurring as a three as well. The total risk figure, therefore, is nine.

The aim of rating the risks is to allow you to decide which ones you're going to plan for. There's no hard-and-fast rule for this—the risks you choose to plan for will depend on your own—and the organization's—attitude to risk. Typically, though, you wouldn't plan for risks that are extremely unlikely to occur, unless they were likely to be catastrophically severe. Equally, there may be some risks that are much bigger than the project itself, and for which you probably don't need to plan—for example, the risk of a complete evacuation of the city you work in because of a terrorist threat. On the other hand, if you're working for the Defense Department, that might well be a scenario you need to plan for!

Let's assume for the moment that you're going to plan for any risks that you rated as extremely likely to occur and for the more severe risks that were less likely to occur. In this case, this approach translates to risks with a rating of approximately ten or more. Now you need to come up with plans for what you'll do if any of these risks become realities.

The ideal here is that you decide on a course of action—a response to each risk—ahead of time. These plans to offset the impacts of the issues are called **mitigation plans**. The key advantages of mitigation plans are that they allow for much higher quality project planning, and they allow you to make the preparations necessary to overcome the issues when they arise.

As an example, let's think back to the first risk example we discussed above, where we didn't have enough content and pictures to complete the site. The mitigation plan for this risk could include convincing the customer to hire a marketing person to provide the content, or to have a member of our own team taking on the task (with an associated project cost, of course, as this task was not included in the initial plan). We might even choose to highlight the risk to the customers early, so they, too, can set aside enough time to complete some preparation in advance, and address the issue successfully if it arises.

 ### The "Do Nothing" Mitigation Strategy

It's perfectly acceptable to decide that no mitigation is required for a given risk. You can choose to do nothing—and simply accept the consequences—if the risk becomes reality. Regardless, it's still important to consider each risk and decide what to do about it ahead of time. This approach will save time and stress later if the risks rear their ugly little heads.

# Representing the Plan

With all the work we've done so far, you'll be pleased to hear that the time has come to represent your project plan. In the next section, we'll look at specific tools and formats you can use to create your plan, but right now, we're going to explore the elements your project plan needs to contain, and how you should represent and communicate it to the people involved in your project.

First of all, let's just reiterate that the *schedule is not the plan.* The schedule represents a group of timings that you're going to try to hit. The total project plan comprises literally everything you have done in the project's Planning phase.

The key aspects that your project plan should cover are:

**deliverables and milestones**
> the items you're actually going to deliver, broken down into logical, manageable chunks

**schedule**
> the goals that will be achieved on given timings, based on the estimates you've compiled

**assumptions and constraints**
> the circumstances or factors you've assumed to be true, and that you've identified as limitations, combined to explicitly state the framework or context you're operating within

**risk management plan**
> the risks you've anticipated, and the steps you'll take to mitigate them if they materialize

Don't forget all the work you've already done on the Project Initiation Document (discussed in Chapter 2). Depending on the project, it may well be sensible to reiterate the reasons why you're undertaking the project, as well as the objective, the high-level deliverables, and the success criteria.

At the very least, you should make sure that you personally refer to that Initiation Document frequently, to make sure you're staying true to the reasons why the project was begun. It's very easy to get caught up in making the project happen while moving further and further away from actually delivering the promised value.

### Assumptions and Constraints

Detailing the project's assumptions and constraints is important because it provides context for the work. Whenever you work with someone else, you both bring loads of background understanding, past experience, and associated assumptions to the job. The point of flagging the assumptions and constraints is to nail down the project's context.

As an example, in the web site design project, perhaps the customer has presumed that you'll not only provide the technical underpinning for the web site, but also the content, pictures, and branding. You, on the other hand, have found in the past that clients want to retain complete control of any text or imagery on the web sites that you build for them.

Putting this assumption down in writing right at the beginning of the project should hopefully cause it to become a topic for discussion, so that the plan (and budget estimates) can be adjusted if this service is needed. By the same token, even if this assumption isn't discussed, and this particular point becomes an issue later, when the project's being executed, you'll have documentation outlining the assumptions and constraints you were operating under, rather than little more than a confused idea that "something's gone wrong." This will make tackling the problem head-on with the people involved much easier, and more effective.

An example of a common constraint on technical projects might be that the project team has to operate within the existing technical infrastructure. Hence, designing a system that would only work on Windows when the client's systems are all Linux based would be purposeless.

### Beware Back-of-an-envelope Plans!

Naturally, your first attempts at planning may well be rough. Some of the most successful projects in the world started as scribbles on the back of an envelope, a cigarette pack—even an airsick bag!

There's nothing wrong with this, so long as you make it obvious—and keep in mind—that these plans are rough. Problems usually arise when you take a back-of-an-envelope plan and try to make it look professional.

Perhaps you're just trying to get the plan into an electronic format. So you fire up some project management software (yes, you're probably thinking of the same product I am) and start inputting your scribbles. Then, the software demands more and more information from you: start dates, durations, end dates, dependencies. Your rough plan didn't have this detail ... but all you really want is to be able to show the plan, right? What's the harm in just filling in your best guess so you can do so?

Next, your boss calls. She's interested in seeing what the project schedule looks like, so you show her the Gantt chart that the software has produced for you. She's pleased and prints a copy to show her boss.

In your next project review or board meeting, you realize that something terrible has happened: because the plan *looked* good, everyone has assumed that it is both complete and accurate. People are now holding you to the project plan that was written on the back of an envelope simply because it *looks* like it was properly estimated, the dependencies were worked out, and the contingency was carefully added.

The moral of the story? If your plan is rough, make it look rough. I'm not advocating that you photocopy the envelope and hand it round (although that might not be a bad idea!), but that you should consider the impact of the format you choose to present your plan. People almost always assume that a plan that looks professional is also accurate. You may be better off presenting a plan that looks less snazzy, but won't be mistaken for a finished product.

# Tools and Best Practices

Now that we've got a grip on the steps involved in the Planning phase, let's look at a number of different tools and best practices that'll help you as you're planning the project. These tools can be used as required during the project—and they all work well together, so feel free to use whichever tools you prefer whenever you need them!

## The Work Breakdown Structure

A **Work Breakdown Structure** (WBS) is a representation of the scope of the project. It comprises a tree structure that hierarchically represents the project and its component deliverables. A WBS for your project should show 100% of the scope and the deliverables—literally everything that has to be delivered for your project.

To construct a WBS, start with the overall project and break it into component deliverables. Then, break each deliverable into its component parts. You should keep breaking the parts down into smaller levels of detail until the pieces are both achievable and manageable. My personal rule of thumb for this task is that the smallest nodes should comprise deliverables that won't take longer than two or three days to achieve. Equally, you don't want to plan milestones that take mere hours to complete, since such will err into the realm of personal productivity (your own to-do list), rather than constituting true project planning.

A WBS can be represented in a number of ways—I've seen them created in everything from Powerpoint and Visio to Omnigraffle. Choose software that you're comfortable with, and that allows you to draw boxes and arrows quickly, or offers inherent tools for creating hierarchical diagrams.

Once you've become used to drawing WBS diagrams, you may find that you can just as easily plot them on paper and turn them into lists of deliverables in normal text. I'd strongly recommend you at least always start with a hierarchy, though, or else you can too easily find yourself creating lists of tasks rather than hierarchies of deliverables. Figure 3.3 shows a WBS.

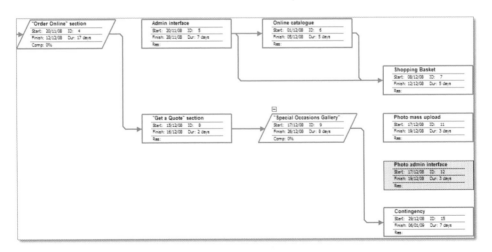

Figure 3.3. An example WBS

# The Gantt Chart

A Gantt chart is the diagram most people think of when they think of the words "project plan." In fact, it's just a way of representing the project schedule in a particular type of bar chart.

Traditionally, it lists the tasks involved in the project on the left-hand side, with bars representing each tasks's duration overlaid on a calendar to the right. As we have already discussed, it's better to plan deliverables than tasks, but we can still use the Gantt chart to identify which deliverables will be worked on when.

I've created an example Gantt chart for our cake shop web site example, which you can see in Figure 3.4. Here, you can see that I've indicated only the true dependencies. The plan does look a little unrealistic, however, since many of the tasks that are currently shown to be taking place in parallel are actually going to be worked on sequentially by our team members. If I were going to use this chart to communicate the schedule for the project, I'd probably make an assumption that stages could not be worked on concurrently, and I'd make the stages dependent on each other.

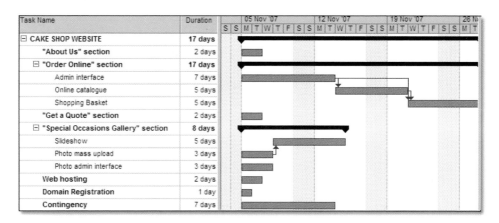

Figure 3.4. An example Gantt chart before resources are allocated

Traditional project management techniques would have you assign each deliverable to the team members who'll be working on it, then perform what's called **resource leveling**. This is the process by which you identify that some people in your team have a daily workload of 200%, whereas others are operating at 20% of capacity. The idea is that, once you've identified these discrepancies, you can reallocate tasks to those who are underutilized, taking some of the pressure off those who are overutilized.

The reality with modern knowledge work, however, is that specific skills are usually required for particular tasks. Reallocating coding work to your design specialist isn't very likely to speed up the project (it might even cause a revolt!). But perhaps more realistically, bringing someone into the team for two weeks when there's intensive coding to be done may also slow the project down rather than speed it up.[2]

If you're in a position to reallocate work to any individual in your team, resource leveling might be a useful approach for you. Alternatively, the best approach might be to set up the project so the team members disseminate the work among themselves. Indeed, this is one of the key tenets of some agile development processes, such as Scrum,[3] and often leads to team members feeling much more ownership for the work they do.

My preferred approach to resource allocation and leveling is to manage these functions on a short-term, rolling basis within the team. Team members can often figure out much smarter ways of helping each other than you can predict weeks ahead of time on your own. We'll talk more about this concept later in the chapter, when we consider the Executing phase of the project loop.

Obviously, if the initial plan proves that you need an extra programmer, designer, or CSS guru, then you probably want to think about expanding your team. However, that need will probably be obvious from the initial schedule you prepare, so you needn't go the resource leveling route.

## Plan Reviews

More a technique than a tool, plan reviews help you to keep your plan alive. A plan review is a short meeting (of not more than 30 minutes) in which you review the project plan with a group of people. I recommend that you conduct separate plan reviews for different groups of people. For example, your project team will have different interests from the project's key stakeholders, and from the project board.

---

[2] This particular subject has already been covered eloquently and thoroughly by Fred Brooks in *The Mythical Man Month* (Addison Wesley, 1975). If you're working in the computing or Web industry, and have never read this book, it's definitely worth the time.

[3] http://en.wikipedia.org/wiki/Scrum_(development)

A plan review consists of taking people through the plan at a high level, and only going into the detail that's relevant to them. Your key stakeholders, for instance, may predominantly be interested to know when you will want their involvement. The project board is going to be more interested in when the key decisions will need to be made.

Without plan reviews, confusion may arise about what the team's working on, and how the project's progressing. Take advantage of these meetings as opportunities to clear up any confusion and to deal with misunderstandings head-on.

## Dealing with Set Deadlines

Ideally, you'll work out how long a project's going to take, having gathered estimates, added contingency, and considered the risks, then defined the schedule and derived the estimated project deadline. The sad reality is that often, projects don't work out this way.

We've all been in a situation where we're given a project *after* senior management has announced that it will be delivered by June 1st. After all, it's the "Next Big Thing," and it's essential for the company's success. And they're showing stunning leadership by letting everyone know that they're not only going after this goal, but that they're doing so aggressively.

Does this sound familiar? As a project manager, you're very likely to have to deal with this kind of situation. You'll find yourself in the midst of a project for which no planning has been done, but a final deadline has already been set. Not only that, but the assumption is that you can deliver the moon on a stick *and* the sun in a paper bag by that deadline.

So what do you do? First, work out how much trouble you're in. Break down the deliverables, gather the estimates, and decide how much contingency you'd have liked to have. You work out that the realistic deadline for the Next Big Thing project is actually December 1st.

But now what? How can you convince management that you need an extra six months in the project plan?

If you're in a wonderful, supportive work environment, you may choose to tackle this issue head-on. Go and explain that the deadline is unachievable, that you simply can't make it. I predict one of two things will happen:

1. Management will replace you with someone who claims they can deliver the project on time.

2. Management will decide this is a cunning tactical ploy to get more budget or resources, and will start throwing more cash and people at you.

The good news is that the guy setting the unrealistic deadline probably doesn't understand the detail of the project. If he did, he wouldn't be setting unrealistic deadlines, right? Right.

So why is this good news? Because all you have to do to go from being depressed because you're chairman of a train-crash-in-waiting, to being the superhero project manager is to remember the balance quadrant.

After all, you understand that you can't do everything with nothing. You're already working under a time constraint, but the other three factors (quality, cost, and scope) are yours to play with. Work out what you *can* achieve by June 1st, and what you need to get there. Then ask for it. Well, if you're smart, you'll probably ask for a little bit more, and management will negotiate down to what you actually need.

 **Illustrating the Crunch**

One way of making the impossibility of the set deadline really come alive for folks who just don't understand is to write the project deadline at the far right of a whiteboard, and work backwards, detailing the high-level tasks that need to be achieved. It will soon become apparent that everything can't be squeezed into the available time, and then you can have a reasonable discussion about what *can* be done.

The most important point is to take the emotion out of the discussion. Get everyone to calm down and face reality, making it about what needs to be done, rather than the emotional reaction of a boss who's being told she can't have what she wants, and a team that's being asked to achieve the impossible.

People who throw unrealistic deadlines around often don't really understand the implications of what they're asking for. You could try to educate them, or you could just come up with a better plan. Define what's doable in the time frame, get the resources you need, and then build it. By the time you've delivered the basic functionality that *is* possible, your customers might have realized that they don't really *need* all the bells and whistles they were asking for in the first place.

# Executing

The Executing phase of the project life cycle is all about doing the work—creating the product. It's where many new project managers feel most comfortable, since they've come from being part of the project team. Nevertheless, there are still some key issues you'll need to look at from a project management perspective.

## Let Your Team Have Ownership

For me, there's really just one rule for the Executing phase of the project:

*Each and every deliverable needs to have an owner.*

Each and every deliverable or milestone, each page that needs to be built, each database that must be configured, each design that must dazzle, needs to be owned by one person. That individual is personally *responsible* and *accountable* for making it happen.

That's not to say that each deliverable is only worked on by one person, but that there has to be someone in the team who feels committed to getting that design created, page written, or feature built. That person will coordinate the work of the others involved, escalate issues to the project manager if it looks like things are going off-track, and ask for help when it's needed.

This approach may seem a bit onerous. You might be worrying that it's too much pressure to put on your team. After all, you're the project manager—you're the one who's meant to have the responsibility, right? Think about the times when you've been happiest at work. Weren't those times when you had control over the outcome of the work you were doing? When someone showed enough trust in you to give you ownership for a project, but also enough support to help you do it? Giving people responsibility isn't a burden, it's freedom.

# The Link to Personal Productivity

Twinned with the idea of giving people ownership for deliverables is the concept of personal productivity. If you're giving people the responsibility to get a job done, you also need to give them the freedom to do it their own way.

If you ever find your project plans resembling a to-do list more than a set of deliverables and estimates, stop and take a step back. Planning your project is about working out what needs to be delivered, not dictating to your team the minor detail of how they should get the job done.

There are a number of great books and resources about time management, prioritizing, and personal productivity. For some pointers, check out Appendix B. In short, let your people get their work done their way.

# Tools and Best Practices

There are a number of tools and best practices that can help us through the Executing phase.

## Adding Ownership to Your Existing Plans

By this point, you already have a plan. The next step is to add ownership to the mix. I recommend you do this on a rolling basis—assign ownership to the pieces of work that you and your team will be focusing on for the next two or three weeks (it can be difficult to make good ownership choices for work to be completed further out than this).

After all, you don't know whether Alex will have been having a hard time getting his head around the database design, or Sandy will have finished the design much faster than expected. Keep things as flexible as possible while keeping the project going.

If you have a strong, well-gelled team, you might find it's best to let the team distribute work among themselves. This way, people can stretch themselves, knowing that the entire team is behind them, and will help out if they come unstuck. However, if your team isn't working well together, or it's the first time these particular people have worked together, letting team members decide how to distribute the work can cause extra, and unnecessary, anxiety.

## Stand-up Meetings

**Stand-up meetings** are exactly what the name implies: meetings in which each person stands up in front of the other attendees to give a brief update about what they're doing. Depending on the type of work you're doing, you might want to conduct these meetings daily, or slightly less frequently, though it's unlikely you'll want to do them less often than once every two or three days, because when you meet less frequently, it becomes hard to keep the meetings short and sweet.

As the team members stand up, they give an update on what they've achieved, and what they'll be doing next, and they highlight any issues or opportunities they've faced.

### Making Next Steps Stick

One effective way of making sure that team members know what they need do after the meeting is to leave sticky notes and pens in the center of the table, so that team members who have a next step to pursue can just write it down and stick it on their screen or to-do list when they get back to their desks.

### Team Size

Stand-up meetings reinforce another great practice: keeping your team size small. Groups of more than six or seven people have been found to have difficulty operating as a true team. The ideal team size is probably no more than seven or eight.

This doesn't mean that you can never work on a project that requires more than seven or eight people. It merely means that when your team becomes larger than this, you should break into subteams.

If you ever find your legs getting tired because you're trying to get updates from twenty people in a stand-up meeting, you definitely need to invest in the subteams principle! In fact, upon examining your team, you may find that your people have already organized themselves into the most effective groupings—all they need from you is the structural change to start having meetings separately. As the project manager, you may end up attending multiple update meetings, but at least the entire team won't be tied up in an overly long meeting each time!

Stand-up meetings are a great way to keep everyone in the team up to date on the project's progress. More importantly, they can be a great way to identify overlaps between people's work, problems that other team members could help with, or the fact that someone is too busy (or not busy enough—it does occasionally happen!) and that work needs to be redistributed.

You might want someone to take notes, but the most important issue is to make sure that people walk away from the meeting knowing their next steps.[4] In other words, they leave the meeting knowing the tasks they need to go and do now, whether it's to help Rada out with that CSS bug, or to give Selim some extra testing to do as he's finished coding early.

# Controlling

The Controlling phase of the project life cycle is all about understanding how you're doing, tracking your progress, and adapting to changing circumstances.

## Are You on Track?

*"Are you on track?"* is probably the question you will be asked most as a project manager. Everyone wants to know whether the project's deliverables are going to be delivered on time and, if not, what you're doing about it.

It's important, therefore, to be able to answer this question for yourself first!

We've already done most of the hard work in this regard. When we were planning the project, we planned deliverables, not tasks. This means that we are able simply to track whether something is completed or not, rather than worrying about the percentage of each task that's complete. During execution, we've given ownership of discrete deliverables to just one person, so that individual is the ultimate authority on whether or not we're on track to deliver that element on time.

Most importantly, we have broken down our deliverables to a level of detail that's fine enough to ensure that we're always going to know—to within a day or two—whether we're on track. If a deliverable isn't on time, we'll only be off-target by a day or two, since that's the total time allocated to any task. This is much better

---

[4] Usually, you're going to be a good choice for note-taker, since the others in the team are likely focused on reporting back and problem-solving together.

than waiting three weeks to realize that we not only are we three weeks late, but that it will take another two weeks to actually deliver a piece of work!

# Measuring Deliverables

Measuring deliverables is a simple matter of asking "is it done?" For this to be effective, though, we need to make sure that both the project team and the customer have the same understanding of what "done" means.

As an example, let's go back to our cake shop web site project. One of the key pieces of functionality was a slideshow designed to share photos of wedding, birthday, and other custom cakes with customers who might want to order similar cakes for themselves.

Tony, a developer in your team, has taken ownership for the creation of the slideshow functionality. This functionality was broken into three key deliverables:

- displaying a single photo
- transitioning from one photo to the next
- adjusting the settings (faster, slower, category selection)

You've checked in with Tony, and all seems to be going well. He's demonstrated the different functions, asking for advice on a few points, and getting help from yourself and Matteo, the interaction designer.

The problem comes at the stand-up meeting the day *after* Tony finished work on the slideshow. He reports at the stand-up meeting that he's intending to spend the day "working the kinks out of the system." You're surprised—after all, you'd seen the functionality demonstrated.

You ask Tony what's up. He explains that the slideshow does work, it's just he hadn't actually been building any tests as he coded, so yesterday afternoon when he started playing around with the finished slideshow, he found a bunch of errors.

The issue here is that Tony thought "done" meant "it's been coded," but you thought it meant "coded, tested, and ready to go." Since you had this difference in your minds from the very beginning of the development, it's affected everything—the estimates that Tony gave you, the way he approached the task, and the questions you were asking to judge whether things were on track or not.

Neither definition is right or wrong, but there are obvious implications. If we take Tony's definition, there needs to be a load of testing and quality assurance built into the project plan at a later stage. If we were using your definition of "done," Tony probably would have given longer estimates in the first place.

Essentially, it's important to make sure you're clear from the outset about what you'll define as "done." Otherwise, you might encounter some nasty surprises as you work through your project.

# Measuring Everything Else

Measuring deliverables is the step that probably gives you the most important indication of how the project's going—it tells you how much of the scope has been delivered. On the other hand, we know that there are three other factors that matter just as much: time, cost, and quality.

Project management practitioners use a system called **Earned Value Management** (EVM) to measure the value delivered (earned value) to date against what was planned. If you're working in an environment where EVM is routinely used, it's worth investing the time to understand the intricacies of this system.

However, if you're mainly going to be communicating with people who aren't already familiar with EVM, you may find you spend more time explaining the measures you're using than actually communicating the value delivered to date.

I find that the following three measures can give a good indication of how the project's going:

1. **scope delivered**

   Which deliverables have been completed?

2. **the percentage time that's passed versus time planned**

   Given the scope completed, are we early, on time or late according to the original plan?

3. **budget used to date**

   It's usually smart to compare this value both to the scope delivered ("If we've already spent half the budget, have we delivered half the scope?") and time that's passed ("If we're halfway through the project timings, how much of the budget have we spent?").

Exactly how you choose to illustrate your progress is up to you, but you'll probably find that different ways of representing how the project's going will be useful for sending different messages to various stakeholders. For instance, you might take your Gantt chart and color all the deliverables that came in on time green, and make those that were late red. This color coding will highlight the particular pieces of scope that are proving problematic.

Budget is almost always best represented as a percentage of the overall budget used. You may find that you need to spend a lot up-front to guarantee the end results of a project—and that's something the customer should be made aware of at the outset of the project. But even the most trusting customer is going to be concerned about a project that's used 50% of its budget and only delivered 10% of the desired product.

Quality, on the other hand, is much more difficult to measure with a generic method. Part of your role as the project manager is to define how quality will be assured and measured. For instance, in a software engineering project, you might focus on what percentage of the code has been tested, or how many of the bugs that were found have been fixed; in a construction project, there may be tests to determine strength of the structure. In many projects, there's also an aesthetic dimension—whether the end product looks and feels as if it's of high quality.

### Resisting the Spiral Out of Control

Every year an appalling percentage of projects undertaken in both the private and public sector go over budget, fail to deliver what was promised, or deliver something late or subpar. As project manager, your role is not only to do everything you can to make your project a success, but also to act as an early-warning system if things are going wrong.

It's much better for your company or organization if you realize early that a project will fail to deliver what's needed. Whether you notice that the budget is being used up much faster than anticipated, or that the scope is overambitious given the time allocated, you need to flag the issue immediately, and deal with it. The worst situation a project can be in is the throwing-good-money-after-bad point—when the organization is continuing to invest even though the costs far outweigh the initially conceived benefits, simply because too much has already been spent for the project to be canceled outright.

I'm a firm believer that the mark of a great project manager is knowing when to press ahead to make the project happen, and when to hold up your hands and say, "The best thing we can do is stop."

## Risks, Issues, and Bugs

If you're not on track, it probably means that one of your risks has materialized. Risks are risks when they are still just potential problems that haven't arisen yet. Once a risk is realized, project management-speak deems it to be an **issue**.

Issues exist at the project level. If you're from a technical or production background, it can be very easy to confuse issues with bugs or defects, but issues are different from bugs. Bugs are technical errors—a system failing to behave in the way you intended. Defects are product errors—an aspect that fails to meet quality standards. Issues are risks that have come to life; they're problems that mean you can't carry on with the project as planned. This doesn't necessarily mean that you have to stop the project completely; it may just be that you need to adapt your direction or your methods a little.

Luckily, you've already planned for those risks that you felt deserved consideration. If any of these have become issues, the great news is that you have a ready-made plan for dealing with them. You may also have encountered other issues—either risks that you didn't identify, or risks that you identified but chose not to create mitigation plans for.

You'll be able to deal with most issues within the project team, and occasionally with help or input from a key stakeholder who has the right expertise or perspective. Sometimes, though, you'll have an issue that's so severe that it needs to be taken to the project board for a decision. Typically, such problems arise when the issue has such serious cost, quality, scope, or time implications that the sponsor of the project needs to be consulted.

For instance, imagine that you encounter a risk that means there's a 50-50 chance that the project might overrun its estimated time frame by six months. The estimated cost of this late delivery would be $200,000—that's the cost of the extra resources needed in those six months, as well as the lost opportunity (if the project had been released on time, there would have been additional sales, lower running costs, and so on). You could eliminate the risk by spending $100,000 now. How do you make this decision?

The reality is that the implications of this business decision are such that you *must* involve your project board. Your role is to make sure the board members understand the situation, the risks, and the associated costs. If your project board members and sponsor have been picked carefully, they will be at the right level in the organization to make the decision about whether to spend the $100,000 up-front, or to wait it out and risk the delay with its associated cost implications.

 **Knowing When to Consult the Board**

My personal litmus test for whether the project board needs to be consulted is to imagine that the worst case scenario arises. If it did, and I reported the situation in my regular status updates, would the board be accepting or outraged?

The answer depends on the context of your project. The example of the potential $200,000 delay cost versus the up-front investment of an additional $100,000 seems significant enough to warrant board involvement, but on a $10 million project, this sum may be small enough to lose down the back of the proverbial sofa without anyone realizing.

Imagine the board members hear about the situation after the fact—if they would be upset about not being involved, take the decision to them.

## Verification Versus Validation

Throughout the Executing and Controlling processes, you'll constantly be verifying the fact that you're creating the deliverables that you planned to create. **Verification** is simply the process of checking that you've built what you intended.

Validation is a separate matter. **Validation** is checking that whatever you're delivering is actually going to deliver the promised value. Validation is what brings you to change course mid-project, despite the fact that you're delivering everything on time, within budget, and to the correct scope and quality.

The average project manager thinks that his or her role is to make the project happen as smoothly as possible. His or her focus is verification—to make sure that the team is building what was promised.

Great project managers distinguish themselves by caring more about the point of the project than anything else. They care about delivering what the customer really needs—not necessarily the product, which can easily become the focus, but the value that underlies it. Validation is their watchword.

# Looping Back to Plan

Most of the time during the Controlling phase, you'll find yourself making minor adjustments to the plan. It will rarely be necessary to restart the planning process from the beginning. Generally, you'll find yourself doing some work (executing), identifying whether you're on track (controlling), making some minor adjustments (planning), and then continuing on working again.

Occasionally, you might find that a serious rethink is needed, in which case you should consider using more of the planning process we discussed earlier in this chapter. If this happens, make sure that you involve your team and your stakeholders. It's easy when you're under pressure to try to do it all yourself, but this is more likely to cause further issues and delays than to get it done faster, because people haven't been properly consulted.

# Tools and Best Practices

Let's look in a bit more detail at the tools and best practices that can help you keep track of your projects.

## Issue Lists

**Issue lists** are used to keep track of the risks that have become reality, posing a challenge to your project's progress. The issue list documents issues with your *project*; by contrast, bug lists are concerned with errors in your *product* (the software, web site, or other item that you're building).

The main reason to keep your issue list separate from your bug list is that addressing the items on each list requires very different skillsets. Bugs are typically corrected through coding changes. Occasionally, what's listed as a bug is in fact evidence of a design flaw or misunderstanding, so the resolution is a change in, or clarification of, the design.

Project issues are typically less technical. Often, resolving a project issue is going to depend more on your negotiation skills than your programming ability. Some might even need to be escalated to the project board for a final decision, although as the project manager, you'll usually be asked to provide at least a recommendation of what you think should be done.

If you take a look at the example issue list in Figure 3.5, you'll see the fields that you'd typically expect—a number (for ease of reference), description, priority level (resist the urge to mark everything as HIGH!), owner (the person who's responsible for resolving the issue), a flag to indicate whether the board will need to be involved, next steps or the documented resolution, the date recorded, the target date for resolution, the actual resolution, and the current status. Status should be fairly simple: either Open (that is, the issue has been raised, but nothing's been done yet), WIP (Work In Progress), or Closed (done and dusted).

| # | Description of Risk or Issue | Priority | Owner | Need Board Action? | Next Steps / Resolution | Start Date | Target Date | Resolved Date | Status |
|---|---|---|---|---|---|---|---|---|---|
| 1 | Content deadlines not being met | Med | Kate | No | Kate to pull together workshop to blitz through all the writing | 06-Nov-08 | 10-Nov-08 | | WIP |
| 2 | *scrummycakes.com* domain not available | High | Meri | Yes | Board selected *justdelish.net* from alternatives proposed | 02-Nov-08 | 15-Nov-08 | 11-Nov-08 | Closed |

Figure 3.5. An example issue list from the cake shop web site project

## Adding to Your Planning Tools

Back in the Planning phase, we already created a Work Breakdown Structure (listing all the deliverables, broken down into manageable chunks) and a Gantt chart (showing the deliverables against their estimated time lines). During execution, we added ownership details to at least one of these plan representations. During the Controlling phase, we can reuse the same format to indicate when a deliverable has been completed, and whether it was done on time or not.

Although you might not feel like you need to update the plans in order to know whether your project is on track (this is more likely to be the case on simpler, smaller projects), it's worth getting into the habit of doing so. For a start, eventually you will be leading projects that, due to their size and complexity, require more sophisticated tracking. Another reason to update your initial plans is to help you judge the accuracy of your estimates.

The latter benefit can be very useful if you find there's a particular pattern to the delays on your project. If every deliverable is completed just a day later than planned, you might want to consider adding a day to every estimate in the next project (or even to the current one). This assessment might also tell you about how your team is only really performing well under that last-minute pressure, particularly if that last day is heralded by copious consumption of energy drinks and the haggard looks of people who have slept under their desks, if at all!

## One-on-ones

Although you've already instituted stand-up meetings in which the whole team shares their progress, plans, issues, and opportunities, it's still important to catch up with your team members individually on a regular basis. We've all hated working for a manager who paid no attention to the people in the team and spent all their time in idle chat. Show your team the respect they deserve.

Even if we ignore the human impact of having a chat over coffee, there are distinct advantages for your project too. One to one, your people may share more of their apprehensions or concerns with you. The skeptics in your team are going to be the first to notice smoke on the horizon, so listen to them. Equally, they may be more likely to share the great idea that's been knocking around in the back of their heads for weeks, or to let you know that they might have a bit of extra capacity to help Selim out with that database configuration.

Learning to deal with people factors rather than the elegant, logical simplicity of technology can be a bit of a rough ride at first, but soon it will become second nature to you.

# Summary

First up in this chapter we considered the Planning phase of the project life cycle. We talked about the different reasons to plan, chief among them being the fact that planning helps you to understand your project better, and to communicate aspects of it to others. We then considered what to plan (deliverables, not tasks!), and how to plan, by following this six-step process:

1. Break the project into pieces small enough to work with.

2. Identify dependencies.

3. Estimate how long each piece will take.

4. Add some contingency.

5. Consider the risks.

6. Represent the plan in a format that the team, project board, and stakeholders will understand and follow.

We then looked at the Executing phase, which is probably the project life cycle phase we're all most comfortable with. We talked about making sure that each deliverable is owned by someone in the team and also about the links between the project and personal productivity.

*"Are you on track?"* is the key question to be answered in the Controlling phase of the project life cycle. In identifying how to answer this question, we also realized that a precise definition of "done" or "complete" is needed before we can really control our projects. We talked about how to measure not only scope, but also time, budget, and quality. We discussed risks and issues, and explored the fact that risks are potential problems, but issues are real; we also made the distinction between an issue (at the project level) and a bug (at the product level). We also touched on the difference between verification (did I build what I said I would?) and validation (have I built what is really needed?).

At each phase of the project life cycle, we investigated the tools and best practices that will help you ensure team members are on-track, keep stakeholders informed, chart your progress, and achieve the project's goals.

In the next chapter we will look at how to keep the project running smoothly.

# 4

# Keeping It Smooth

In this chapter, we're going to look at the skills that help you keep everything running smoothly. First, we'll consider the importance of communication and collaboration, and discuss some tips to help you communicate effectively and foster a collaborative environment for your team.

We'll then look at managing change (one of the biggest challenges for any project manager!), providing you with tools and techniques to help you make the right decision as often as possible—and to recover gracefully from any missteps.

## Communication and Collaboration

**Communication** is about imparting and receiving information, while **collaboration** is about working together as effectively as possible. In this section, we'll not only talk about how to keep the project's stakeholders informed, but also about how to help your project team members work together both within the team, and with the stakeholders, customers, and management.

# Communication

Communication is an everyday part of everyone's life—so why does it deserve particular attention in project management? Good communication can make a project, just as bad communication can destroy it. If people involved in your project are confused, trouble is on the horizon.

The only thing worse than confusion is when there is absolute clarity ... over different versions of events! If you and your team members believe that installing the new computer system and software is what your project is all about, but the customer thinks you have promised to eradicate all paperwork, sooner or later this mismatch of expectations is going to become a *big* problem.

Being able to communicate effectively is a key skill for any project manager. Communication isn't just talking and emailing, though—good communication involves three key aspects: form, method, and content.

## Form

In your previous interactions with people, you'll already have experienced the various forms of communication. You've undoubtedly experienced **interpersonal communication**: one on one communication, including conversations, arguments, and negotiations. You've probably seen or given **presentational communication**, typically in one to many situations, where one person at a time communicates to a group. And you'll know all about many to many communication, which ranges from the productive team discussion to the mini-riots in which both sides become increasingly emotional (think of discussing politics around the dinner table).

Each of these forms of communication can involve one- or two-way communication. In most situations, you'll want interaction, so you'll probably need two-way communication. Occasionally, though, you'll just want to impart information, in which cases one-way communication may be just fine.

It's important to remember that the form of communication isn't the only element that will determine how interactive communication will be—even if you set up a meeting with the intent that it to be a two-way discussion, other factors can cause one-way communication to occur. For instance, if one group has a great deal of power over the other (as in the case of student-teacher meetings), the less powerful group may be hesitant to speak.

Being able to judge which form offers the best way to communicate in a particular situation is one of the skills that a project manager must develop. It's a talent that's very much part of the art of project management, rather than the science, since picking the best form may depend just as much on intuition as on the facts available.

 ## Choosing the Right Form of Communication

If you're finding it difficult to work out the best form of communication to use, try thinking about the best-case scenario, and the worst-case scenario, that could result from your use of different forms of communication. For instance, if you tell Tim off in front of the team for being late, the best that could happen is that he'll hang his head and apologize; the worst is that he'll get angry, bear a grudge, and spend the rest of the day updating his CV and uploading it to job sites rather than doing any work. On the other hand, if you talk to him about it one-to-one, the worst-case scenario may still eventuate, but it's less likely, as you won't be embarrassing him in front of all his colleagues.

That said, there are some general guidelines that you can use:

**If it's personal, individual, or sensitive, deal with it one-to-one.**

Whether Jim's ongoing illness is causing project delays, you are concerned that Ankur won't want to work on the new burger chain contract because of his religious beliefs, or simply that Alex is being promoted, these situations—and others like them—should be dealt with individually first, in a one-to-one meeting, rather than in a group setting.

**Separate meetings that have different purposes.**

If you want to update stakeholders on the progress of the project, inviting them to the team meeting in which team members will discuss the achievability of the project deadline isn't smart. Run a separate, short presentation for the stakeholders, and make time for a lengthier team meeting to encourage open discussion—without senior management in the room getting upset.

**Choose the appropriate format for your purpose.**

Consider what you're trying to achieve, and choose the best form for that purpose. Presentations are good for informing groups of people of progress, a decision, or an upcoming change. They aren't a good format for discussion—if you want two-way communication, hold a meeting instead. Similarly, turning the team meeting into a series of one-to-one discussions with individual members isn't a productive use of anyone's time except yours, so schedule mini-meetings instead, or just catch up over coffee!

## Method

Every day, we're faced with multiple decisions about which communication method we should use—phone, email, voicemail, instant messenger, letter, fax, meeting, video conference, audio conference, desktop sharing, text message (SMS), podcasts, video casts, blogs, wikis, and more.

When you're choosing a method of communication, there are some basic considerations that you should review, such as whether the method promotes a **push** approach (that is, information is pushed out to the receiver, as it is via an email or presentation), or a **pull** approach (in which the person who needs information asks for or collects it when it's needed, as is the case with blogs, noticeboards, and so on). Also keep in mind that some methods support different forms of communication better than others. For instance, email is a good method for one-to-one and one-to-many communication, but terrible for many-to-many discussions or conversations.

Possibly the most complex consideration when you're selecting a method of communication involves assessing people's expectations of that method. Some people view email as a high priority, and will deal with it accordingly; others believe that it's a low-urgency form of communication, and that if something's important, people will pick up the phone and actually talk to one another.

As an example, my personal preference for the hierarchy of communication methods can be explained like this. The best way to get hold of me is always email. Instant messenger is probably a close second, but unlike some people, I'm not logged in all the time, so an email still may be read faster. I let my phone go to voicemail more often than not, and will frequently check my email before I access my voice messages.

Faxes get routed to my email inbox, but it can take me weeks to get to real hard copy mail, partly because I travel so much that I'm seldom in the office, and partly because I expect anyone with an important question to email me! Planned face-to-face or virtual meetings (whether they're audio or video conferences) are fine, but unless you send me an electronic invitation at least a week in advance, I'm unlikely to be able to carve out the time for your meeting. Of course, this hierarchy is complex and very personal, so my usual advice to colleagues and acquaintances is just, "The best way to get hold of me is email," rather than a long and involved prescription of preferences!

How does your personal hierarchy of methods compare to this? Is email king for you too, or do you prefer for people to come and talk to you in person, or at least to pick up the phone? Now think of the person who's your opposite in terms of his or her communications preferences. How are that person's preferences different from yours? If you send him or her an email, will it be given a different priority than you intend?

For example, my friend Simone, who's in Human Resources and very much a people person, is uncomfortable with some communication methods, which she views as impersonal. If something's urgent, Simone expects a phone call. Not only that, but that if it's truly urgent, she expects that you will not only leave a voicemail message, but that you'll ring back again if you don't hear from her in an hour or two.

She loves it when people come to her desk to ask her a question, although sometimes if she is getting distracted a lot she'll go and sit in a meeting room to get some work done. She only very occasionally signs on to her instant messenger client and treats all email as low-priority communication. She revels in face-to-face meetings, but rarely schedules them in advance, preferring to grab people on the day and have an impromptu discussion. I'm sure you can imagine how difficult we found it to work together at first!

 **Personal Preferences Prevail!**

Each person's preferences for communication methods are extremely personal. Don't try to impose your preferences on others, but understand theirs so you can communicate more effectively.

The point here is that it's important to understand how these communication preferences will affect your project. It may be worth having a team discussion about communication, to help your team members understand which parties are happy to be interrupted with a request for help, and who would prefer to get an email or an instant message asking them to signal when they have five minutes to talk.

### Communication Preferences Exercise

It can be helpful to conduct an exercise with your team to illustrate the differences in the priorities people place on different communication methods. List the most commonly used methods of communication for your organization or team. Give each person a printed copy of the list, and ask them to rank the methods in order of importance. Then, compare notes. This is a good way of illustrating just how different people's expectations can be!

Of course, you also need to understand the preferences of your key stakeholders and the project board. You might spend hours carefully crafting project status update emails, only to find that the stakeholders are still coming and perching on the edge of your desk, asking you how it's going. You'll get frustrated because it feels like you're repeating yourself, and they'll get frustrated because you keep sending them long emails when all they want is a 15-minute briefing on a Monday morning, so they understand what's going on.

### Technophiles, Take Note!

If your job involves using technology day in and day out, it's easy to forget that it doesn't come as easily to others. Many folks still find electronic communication impersonal, feeling that it's emotionless. Since emails and instant messages lack personal cues, like tone of voice, facial expressions, and body language, they can lend themselves to misunderstandings.

Try consciously to think, "Is responding electronically the right thing to do?"—particularly when a difference of opinion occurs. Hostile email chains can grow very quickly, and sometimes all that's really needed is a judiciously timed phone call to sort things out before the situation escalates out of control.

Sometimes, it'll be enough to decide how key updates and decisions will be communicated (as you did in the communication plan you prepared during the project

Initiation phase), but sometimes, a little trial and error may be in order. Whatever you plan for your current project, you'll find that the experience adds up, and soon you'll be picking the best combination of form, method, and content without much conscious thought.

## Content

In addition to the forms and methods of communication, there's also the question of the actual content—the information you're trying to convey. This may include facts and figures, a project status update, a summary of recent meetings, or a key project decision. But, whatever your content, you need to make sure that you're clear on three issues:

| | |
|---|---|
| **1. purpose** | What are you trying to achieve? |
| **2. structure** | How are you going to present the information? |
| **3. outcomes** | What should the people receiving the information do once they have it? |

When you're considering the purpose of your communication, you need to think about it not just from your point of view, but also from those of your audience. First of all, define what you want to achieve: for example, "update the project board on the project's status." But what do the project board members want? Do they just want to receive the information? Do they want reassurance that the project is on track? Do they want to know if any key decisions need to be made? Or all of the above?

Once you've defined the purpose of the communication both for yourself and your audience, you can focus on structure. What sort of structure will communicate the information most effectively, given the communication's purpose? If the purpose of the project status update is to reassure the project board that the project's on track, you want to make that point obvious as quickly as possible. That's why many people choose "traffic light indicators" for their status updates—anything communicated in green is on track, anything in yellow or orange has issues, and any points that are made in red are in jeopardy. These visual cues mean that the message behind the words is brought to the forefront as quickly as possible.

Most people will finish reading an email, watching a presentation, or sitting in a meeting with one key thought in their heads: "What do you want me to do about it?" You should always answer this question in your communication. Sometimes it will be as simple as recording a list of "next steps" for your team after a team meeting. Other times, you'll need the project board to go away and make a decision about how to proceed, given an issue that has been encountered. Whatever outcome you desire, the more obvious you make it, the more likely you'll be to get it.

 **Next Communication Details**

Sometimes you don't need any action from your audience—especially if the communication was purely informative. In this case, it's smart to round off your communication with information about when the next communication will be scheduled or issued. This reassures people that no further action is needed on their parts, other than turning up to the next meeting or reading the next email.

## Creating the Feedback Loop

It's very easy for us project managers to get focused on how we'll be communicating to the project team, stakeholders, and project board. However, it's just as important to make sure that everyone out there knows how to communicate back to you! You need to know about great ideas, issues popping up on the horizon, and potential risks and opportunities just as much (if not more so!) as stakeholders need to be informed of the project's progress, and the team needs to know when the deliverables are due. The way to achieve these goals is through a feedback loop.

 **Giving the Option of Anonymity**

Sometimes, in particularly political environments, it can be worth creating an "ideas box" into which people can drop slips of paper on which they've explained ideas they've had for your project. If you want to be slightly more high-tech, you could create a web page to allow people to submit their suggestions anonymously. In an environment where being overly negative, realistic, or even just too honest could cost staff members their next promotions, creating these anonymous avenues can be both very important and very valuable.

Depending on the culture of the organization where you're working, you could establish the feedback loop in a number of ways. You might set aside ten minutes of each team meeting to allow people to voice their concerns or share ideas they've had. You could also make a point of having a quick, regular coffee with your key stakeholders, to give them the chance to informally share their ideas, experiences, and expertise. Sometimes, you'll need to actively pursue this interaction, but sometimes, by making clear that your door is open, and dealing constructively with the concerns brought to your attention, you can create an environment where people automatically feel comfortable coming and talking to you.

# Collaboration

Collaboration, although it *requires* excellent communication, is about working together as effectively as possible. As the project manager, most of your interaction with the stakeholders and the project board will focus on communication. However, with the project team, collaboration is the focus: as project manager, you're responsible both for leading the team and for fostering an environment in which the team can collaborate effectively.

Where successful communication primarily relies on a good communication flow, collaboration is about forming relationships. With a new team working on a new project, your team members may feel unsure about each other as well as the new challenges they're undertaking. Even if the individuals have worked together in the past, there may still be aspects of the new project that will introduce uncertainty.

## Turning Groups into Teams

Putting individuals together makes them a group, but only when they can work together effectively will they really be a team. Helping your people to become a team, rather than remaining a group, is one of the most important roles you have as a project manager.

But how do you go about it? First of all, you need to understand how group dynamics work. There is, of course, an entire field of study that deals with organizational psychology and groups in the workplace. Here, we'll look at a simple model that explains the stages that groups go through as they become teams, namely forming, storming, norming, performing, and adjourning. These phases are depicted in Figure 4.1.

Figure 4.1. Forming, storming, norming, performing, and adjourning

In the **forming** stage, group members get to know each other, and start to understand what the point of the group is. In project terms, this stage typically takes place when the team is originally formed, and the Initiating phase is underway. It's a time of information gathering and introductions. At this stage, people are usually still very independent and focused on themselves: what does the project mean for them? What will they be doing?

As project manager, you can help smooth the forming stage by making time to understand your team, and giving them a chance to get to know each other. Encourage the team members to share information about their backgrounds, past experiences, and reasons for wanting to work on the project. Share information about the project they'll be undertaking, but don't overwhelm them with details of exactly what each team member will be doing.

## Start the Project with a Get-to-know-you Session

If possible, bring all the team members together in person at the start of the project. Have everyone introduce themselves and talk a bit about their backgrounds, experiences, and skills. If the team has really never worked together before, you might include some "icebreaking" exercises. Try to build plenty of free time into your session, to allow individuals can get to know each other and build relationships informally.

If you're unable to get everyone together, or if they're working remotely, you should still hold a kickoff meeting. Call everyone on the phone, or into an online chat, and try to get the team talking as much as possible. Encourage everyone to find time after the initial meeting to talk to every other member of the team, whether it's in person, on the phone, or via instant messenger. This time might feel like a lot of initial overhead that's unrelated to the project tasks, but if it makes your team work better together, the up-front investment will definitely pay off later.[1]

The group then progresses to **storming**, where differences of opinion come to the fore. Confrontations about how to proceed with the project, who should decide which deliverables are owned by whom, what the best approaches will be, and what tools should be used, will abound. For those group members who don't enjoy confrontation and conflict, this can be a very painful stage. Others may revel in the perceived competition and push to "win," or have their proposed ideas or methods chosen.

In project terms, storming is most likely to begin during the Planning phase of the project. Depending on the maturity of the individuals on the team, it may involve only a short period of time, but some groups never move out of the storming stage. Since it's definitely not the most productive state for a group to be in, your role as manager is to help the team to achieve consensus and a route forward as soon as possible. The main things to emphasize are tolerance and patience—help people to respect each others' opinions and experience, and to realize that the conflict won't continue forever!

---

[1] You might want to think about videoconferencing, but many people are still a bit uncomfortable with this technology. Judge what you think is best based on people's levels of comfort with the technology.

## Stuck Storming?

Some groups get stuck in the storming stage, and unfortunately, it increases the chances of project failure. If your team is conflict-ridden for a long time, start thinking about what you could do to overcome the problem. Try to work out whether conflict is focused around a particular issue—if so, it might be best to bring it out in the open, and have a brainstorming meeting on that specific topic.

If particular individuals are continually at each other's throats, then try to work out what's going on. Are they simply having a personality clash? Or is there some serious difference of opinion underlying their arguments? You might want to facilitate a discussion, try to tone down the emotion, and focus on the root of the problem. Alternatively, having a quiet word with each individual, stating that you've noticed the problem, and hope that they'll try to be more understanding of each other—and work better together in future—may do the trick.

As a last resort, you might even need to consider removing "bad apples" from the team for the health of the whole.

Next comes the **norming** stage, where group members start to work together more easily. Often, this stage involves agreeing on standard ways of working, tools that will be utilized, and the ways in which issues and conflicts will be dealt with. The group starts to feel more like a team at this stage, with members trusting each other more and starting to help each other more frequently.

## Beware of Groupthink!

There is a danger in the norming stage that the group can become too conformist. It's in such situations that phenomena like **groupthink**—where the group automatically assumes that the idea that the group agrees on must be the best, and ignores outside inputs or different ideas—can surface. It's important to keep an eye out for these kinds of problems, and to address them by actively promoting the consideration of different ideas by the team.

**Performing** is the most productive stage. The group is now truly a team, and together they can achieve much more than they could as a collection of individuals. They rely on each other for help and support, and though this doesn't mean that there's no disagreement, it does indicate that healthy ways of dealing with differing opinions have been developed.

Often, teams acting in the performing stage need very little managing—they can make decisions, allocate work, complete it, and keep track of their progress. This doesn't mean that a project manager is no longer needed, but that you're most likely to be working *with* the team, rather than having to direct them, which might have been necessary in the earlier stages while the group was forming.

The final stage that teams experience is **adjourning**—the team is disbanded, usually when the project is completed. Some even refer to this stage as mourning, since after being in a performing team, individuals feel a real sense of loss on separation. Often individuals will have built up strong relationships with other team members, and may stay in contact long after the initial team has been disbanded.

Team dynamics is one of the trickiest areas for new project managers. Sometimes, your role will require you to get in there and get your hands dirty—deal with conflict, make changes to the structure of the team, and so on. But at other times, the best thing you can do is to do nothing, allowing the natural progression of the cycle to develop the team.

Sadly, there aren't any prescriptions for how long it will take the team to move from one stage to the next, nor how to move a group along. As you gain more experience, you'll become more adept at doing the right thing at the right time, but to start you off, here are some top tips for each stage of the process:

**forming**

Make time for people to get to know each other at the start of the project. Diving straight into the work without making time for this important process means that your team members will remain tentative with each other—they, and the project, won't gain the benefits of their working as a proper team.

**storming**

Accept that conflict is normal and that suppressing it won't move you forward—the disagreements will simply remain simmering beneath the surface. Let team members sort it out, and only step in when things are going too far. Some raised voices can be okay, but screaming insults—or worse—obviously is not.

### norming

It can be tempting to just sit back and enjoy the peace and quiet when the team is involved in this stage. They'll be getting on with their tasks, and generally working well with each other. Your main role is to keep an eye on whether the team is becoming too inwardly focused, or succumbing to groupthink. Also, continue to support relationship building and encourage new ideas at this stage.

### performing

Your primary role here is to preemptively avoid anything that could interfere with the performance of the group. Be a filter for them—don't let anyone (including management!), or anything, bug your team. Take away as much of the administrative burden as you can, and let the team focus on achieving as much as they can together.

### adjourning

Different people will handle the team's break up differently. Accept this, but be sure to celebrate the work that the team undertook together!

## Fostering a Collaborative Environment

As project manager, there's a lot you can do to help create a collaborative working environment for your team. Some of the following tips will be more effective at certain stages of the team development process just discussed, as identified below.

### Encourage relationship building.

People need to build up at least a basic level of rapport before they'll be able to work together well. If at all possible, get the team together in person at the beginning of the project for one or two days. Brainstorm project approaches, run some exercises, and leave plenty of time for individuals to interact with each other one on one. (Forming, Storming)

### Reward collaboration.

Members of your team need to feel that they'll be rewarded for helping each other. These rewards don't need to be anything as big as a salary incentive—simply acknowledging the team member's individual contributions publicly as and when they're made is enough to show the value of their work. You could also encourage your team to thank each other in the team meetings. (Storming, Norming, Performing)

**Discuss communication preferences up-front.**

We talked in the previous section about people having different preferences for the ways they communicate and interact with each other. Discuss these preferences up-front, and let each team member identify his or her preferred method of communication. Create a poster or sheet that reminds everyone that Adam, Rob, and Jas all prefer email, Sinead, Layla, Priya, and Victoire prefer face-to-face meetings, and Li, Arun, and Kai are fine with either instant messenger or telephone. (Forming, Storming)

**Set up a regular team meeting.**

As well as making it easier for you to communicate information to the whole team, team meetings provide a valuable opportunity for discussion and relationship building. Encourage team members to raise concerns, or ask for help from each other in this forum. (Storming, Norming)

**Define an issue reporting and resolution process.**

Accept that there will be differences of opinion, and realize that this is a symbol of a healthy team! Make sure everyone knows how to raise a concern, and how a decision will be made about it. If you agree the process early on, it will be easy to make sure you follow it consistently, and will help people to feel that they've been listened to and treated fairly. (Storming, Norming)

 **Making Time for Soft Work**

It may be difficult to carve out time for these "soft" pursuits. Even people in your group may object, citing that getting on with work is more important than getting to know each other. You need to make time, because an effective team can achieve a lot more than a loosely-coupled group. The time invested in this objective will pay off handsomely in improved productivity.

## Working Remotely

These days, many of us find ourselves working with people who are spread across both time and space—working together in an office is almost a luxury! So how do you collaborate effectively with a team that you might never have met in person? How do you ensure that team works well across multiple locations and time zones?

The first thing to understand is that the same issues matter—it's only the way in which they're achieved that's different. At the end of the day, people are still people. Interpersonal relationships are still important. You can have just as rich a working relationship with someone you only ever talk to over email, instant messenger, and the phone as you do with the person who sits next to you in the office.

Here are some suggestions for helping remote teams to work together more effectively:

**Share *lots* of contact details.**
Create a document that contains your team members' contact details—their names, addresses, phone numbers, fax numbers, email addresses, and instant messenger identities. Add a photo so that people have a picture of who they're communicating with. Make it as easy as possible for people in the team to communicate with each other, and to view each other as real people—not just names behind email messages.

**Pull together a skills matrix.**
Document the skills your different team members have, so that if someone needs help with a particular issue or task, he or she doesn't have to wait until the next team meeting to ask for assistance. This tactic helps to replace the "ask around the office" option that collocated teams have.

**Create group spaces.**
In real offices, a team can grab a meeting room to discuss something at short notice. Try to create the same opportunity in the virtual environment—set up a dedicated teleconference number used just for that team, and create a wiki or bulletin board where updates can be given by team members when an intensive team task is being worked on. If collaborating is made easy, it's more likely to happen.

**Be respectful of time and routine differences.**
In the office, it's obvious when someone isn't working. When team members are working remotely, people need to adjust to each other's routines—an issue that's often further complicated by many freelancers and remote workers working from home offices. Be clear about who works when—if your team members are spread across different time zones, make sure that details of where everyone is, and the current times in those locations, are easily accessible.

**Keeping Track of Time Zones**

Timeanddate.com[2] has a personalized clock tool that allows you to select cities from around the world and have the local time in each city displayed on a single screen. Whenever I work with teams that are spread around the globe, I encourage everyone to use this tool—it can help team members to choose the method of communication that's most appropriate, given the local time of the recipient. For instance, it might be lunchtime for you, but if you need an answer from Paawan (who's 4.5 hours ahead of you) before the end of the day, you'll realize it makes more sense to pick up the phone now, rather than send an email after your lunch break.

**Overdo it personally.**

You need almost to over-invest in relationship building. Often, if you're working with a team whose members are all based remotely, you'll become something of a hub—team members may be more likely to come to you than to go to each other. Become a facilitator—know everyone's strengths, weaknesses, skills, and preferences, and match them appropriately as the need arises.

## Transitioning from Project to Personal Plans

The other big challenge for collaboration is to shift gear from focusing on the project as a whole, to honing in on personal plans—a challenge that requires you to look at the project in a different level of detail. As we discussed during the Planning section of Chapter 3, at a project level, the focus is almost always on the items that are being delivered. But in reality, people actually work on *tasks* day-to-day—they define what's needed to create the deliverable in question, and follow a process to build the components that will combine into the final product.

Although each deliverable should have one (and only one) owner who's accountable for making sure that item is completed, there will, of course, be a need for individuals to work together on different tasks. Being able to effectively define and delegate tasks is something that your team members will need to get used to and become good at.

---

[2] http://www.timeanddate.com/

The process of taking a deliverable and breaking it into the tasks required to achieve it won't be a foreign concept for you. Every day we all decide that we want to achieve something (a goal or deliverable) and work out what we need to do to make it happen. The challenge lies in doing this in such a way that everyone involved understands what's needed, and makes sure that progress is made.

It's at this point that items like project specifications and design documents come into their own. Having a written record of what needs to be achieved can be a very powerful tool for making sure people are working towards the same goal. There are other ways to help ensure that the image you have of what you need to do or build is the same as the picture in your teammates' minds. You might involve the team in informal sketching sessions with just a whiteboard and pen, storyboarding a process or system (such as mapping a customer experience or interaction). For more technical projects, you might want to use UML (Unified Modeling Language), or even mathematical specifications.

The most effective way to communicate the project's components, and explore how they translate into individual tasks, is to take the approach that works for everyone involved. For instance, if you're designing a web site, Adobe Photoshop mockups may be clearer for everyone than code decompositions, unless you only need to communicate with developers who can read code as easily as they can normal prose. Likewise, using UML is only a good idea if everyone involved in the project can easily understand it—you don't want people expending more effort to understand the communication technique than they spend considering the idea you're trying to communicate.

 **Looking Beyond the Team**

Don't forget that it's not just your team members that need to be on the same page in terms of what's being built: consider the customer and end users too. Your team members might all agree on the design and build it, but all your work will be useless if the customer and end users want something else. Define how you will get the initial customer/user requirements at the beginning of the project, and also consider how you will confirm with them along the way that what you're building will meet their needs.

To be honest, there are countless different approaches for helping your team to collaborate. What's important is not that you choose the trendiest or most talked-about one, but that you allow the team to choose the method that will help its members collaborate most effectively. Both the preferences of individuals in the team, and the nature of the project, will need to be taken into account, but the critical thing is that everyone feels comfortable with the method chosen.

## Effective Leadership and Management

A project manager has two roles—one as manager, coordinating the efforts on the project, the other as leader, making sure that the project delivers the right results.

Stephen Covey's *7 Habits of Highly Effective People* illustrates the difference between leadership and management with these lines:

"… envision a group of producers cutting their way through the jungle with machetes. They're the producers, the problem solvers. They're cutting through the undergrowth, cutting it out.

The managers are behind them, sharpening their machetes, writing policy and procedure manuals, holding muscle development programs, bringing in improved technologies and setting up working schedules and compensation programs for machete wielders.

The leader is the one who climbs the tallest tree, surveys the entire situation and yells *"Wrong jungle!"*[3]

Making sure that progress is made as quickly and efficiently as possible while ensuring that everyone's heading in the right direction is a key skill for any project manager.

Paul Hersey and Ken Blanchard developed a model for understanding how people's needs for direction and management differ depending on the situation they're in. In the same way, the style of the manager or leader should change to fit what individuals need most from them.[4] The leadership and management behavior types defined by Hersey and Blanchard are illustrated in Figure 4.2.

---

[3] Stephen Covey, *7 Habits of Highly Effective People*, Simon and Schuster UK Ltd, London 1989.
[4] Paul Hersey, Kenneth Blanchard and Dewey Johnson *Management of Organizational Behavior*, Prentice Hall, New Jersey 2000.

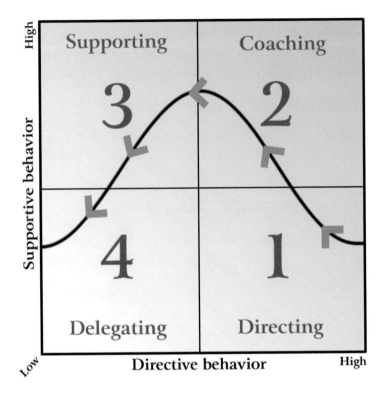

Figure 4.2. Leadership and management behavior types

There are four main styles of behavior leadership and management:

**S1: Directing**

Directing involves close supervision, defining roles and tasks in detail, and telling the team member what to do and how to do it.

**S2: Coaching**

Coaching, which is more interactive, entails helping the team member to come up with his or her own ideas and follow them through, but still required you to define roles and the broad approach.

**S3: Supporting**

With this style, day-to-day decisions (such as which tasks to complete) rest with the team member; the manager participates in those decisions on an as-needed basis.

### S4: Delegating

Wholesale pieces of work are given to the team member to own; that team member chooses if and when to involve the manager.

Team members can be at a variety of developmental levels:

### D1: Low Competence, High Commitment

The team member's keen and motivated, but lacks some of the knowledge or skills required.

### D2: Some Competence, Low Commitment

The team member has some skills, but still needs some help and direction, and may lack motivation.

### D3: High Competence, Variable Commitment

The team member's experienced, and has all the right skills, but might lack the confidence or motivation to just "go it alone."

### D4: High Competence, High Commitment

The team member's experienced, confident and motivated—possibly even more skilled than the manager in the relevant arena.

The diagram Figure 4.2 illustrates how the management style should match the development level of the team member. For instance, a D1 team member ideally requires S1 leadership—the team member is keen, but lacks knowledge or skills, so he or she would require close supervision and direction. The key point here is that it's crucial that you match your management approach to individuals' development levels. Let's look at a couple of examples to illustrate why.

## Example 4.1. Example: S4 to D1

First, let's consider the situation in which a brand new person joins your team. Your project is to develop a web site that collects customer orders, complaints, and queries, and provides the functionality necessary to deal with them. The new guy's role is testing—he's going to be going through the whole site looking for bugs and inconsistencies. On his first day, you show him to his desk, sit him down in front of the computer, and then rush off to an all-day meeting somewhere else.

Why won't this situation work? He's likely to be at D1 (eager, but not really sure of what he should be doing or how) and you're treating him with the S4 style, delegating the entire piece of work to him. The best result you can expect is that you come back to find out that he's worked out vaguely what the web site is about, and has made some notes about not liking the color. The worst-case scenario is that he's annoyed and no longer motivated to do well—you might even find he's not there when you get back!

## Example 4.2. Example: S1 to D4

As a counter example, imagine you're going on holiday for three weeks. While you're away, a fellow project manager will be making sure that your project progresses and that things are on track when you return. Despite the fact that this colleague is arguably more experienced than you, you prepare copious notes and instructions, explaining the most basic concepts of project management in intimate detail.

The most likely outcome is that you will seriously annoy—if not insult—your colleague by treating her like a rank amateur, and she will just keep your project on track in her own way, ignoring your instructions. You'll come back to find that the key things you wanted doing (like making sure the regular status reports go out) haven't happened, and though your project is on track, your working relationship with your colleague is permanently damaged!

Again, the issue here is a mismatch of styles. Your colleague is at a D4 level of capability (she's probably better than you!) and you've been treating her with an S1 style (directing in minute detail). Had you simply delegated the work and asked her nicely to continue the couple of things that were different in your project (that is, matching her D4 capabilities with an S4 style), you'd both be much happier.

Bear in mind that all the people in your team will be at different stages of development. Also remember that they won't be approach all tasks with the same level of capability and confidence—your strongest technical person may need no help at all with technical matters (D4), but she might need a lot more help from you to prepare a presentation for the project board (S1 or S2). Try to predict who's going to need your help and with which tasks, and you'll find it much easier to manage your own time and involvement as well!

# Tools and Best Practices

Let's consider some tools and best practices that will help you keep your communication and collaboration running smoothly.

## Email Etiquette

We all know how to use email. Using email *effectively*, however, is another matter entirely! By introducing a little structure and adopting a few tips, you can drastically improve the efficiency of your email communications:

**Write a good subject line.**

It should be descriptive and specific. For example, "ProjectABC Approval: Final Sign-off Requested by 5pm 29 Nov 08" is better than "Sign Off Please."

**Use cues to indicate the action needed.**

Make clear whether something is just FYI (For Your Information) or whether approval, action, or input is needed. Put the key verb in the subject line.

**Reverse the structure.**

Typically, when we're communicating a recommendation, request, or summary, we assume we need to talk through the background, the process, and the results before getting to the real point of the message. People are busy. Help them out by placing a summary of what you're telling them, or what you need them to do, right at the top of your email, with the details to follow in subsequent paragraphs. Your readers will then have the choice to trust your summary and act, or to read the rest to understand your reasoning.

**If you need something done, set a deadline.**

It's difficult to convey priority well in an email, and the myriad of other tasks that your recipients needs to complete will often take precedence over whatever you ask of them. Setting a reply-by date helps them to focus on getting back to you when you need them to, rather than letting your request drop to the bottom of their to-do list.

**Use lists and bullet points.**

Lists and bullet points are easier to scan than paragraphs, and will allow the people reading your email to get the key points much more quickly.

**Be specific about responsibilities.**

Make it very obvious in your email who's meant to take ownership for a task or next step—put their names in bold or capital letters, so that they can't be missed. Don't leave any next steps undelegated—place a name alongside each one, and if everyone needs to do the task, such as updating the issue list, then say "all." Emails are not a good place to solicit volunteers for a task.

**Keep it short and simple (KISS).**

Emails that are longer than about three paragraphs won't get read. Make sure any point that's actionable is right at the beginning, along with the key information you are imparting.

**Know when to step outside of email!**

Email is a wonderful tool, but sometimes things are better dealt with over the phone, instant messenger, or in person. If emails are flying back and forth, either when you're trying to explain something complex, or when there's a disagreement brewing, consider stepping out to another medium. Don't let things escalate out of control in a nasty email spiral!

## Meeting Standards

Meetings are frequently reviled in the workplace, mainly because people end up sitting through so many meetings that seem pointless. The biggest courtesy you can pay to your colleagues is to make clear the purpose of the meeting up-front, so they can opt out if they aren't needed. There are a range of other tactics you can use to ensure your meetings are always effective:

**Publish an agenda up-front.**

Make sure that everyone knows what will be discussed. An **AOB** (any other business) section is a common inclusion, but your colleagues need to trust that if a discussion arises in which they should be involved, you'll request a separate meeting that involved the right people, rather than making decisions without them.

### PEPS Up Your Meetings

Use PEPS—purpose (why you're having the meeting), end products (what the outcomes will be), and standards (standards you'll adhere to)—to summarize the meeting's objective. Here's an example:

| | |
|---|---|
| **Purpose:** | Plan the annual Christmas party. |
| **End Products:** | Venue, menu, and price are all agreed. |
| | Owner will be assigned to send invitations. |
| | Owner will be assigned to organize decorations. |
| **Standards:** | Be on time. |
| | Meeting will not overrun the allocate time. |
| | Everyone's opinion counts—allow others to speak. |

**Make clear whose attendance is required and whose is optional.**

It's easy to simply invite everyone to every meeting. It's also a lazy approach. Keep the list of "must attend" invitees as small as possible, and only add people to the "optional" list if they truly might be interested in the meeting.

**Pay attention to logistics.**

If the purpose of your meeting is to map out a new business process, holding the meeting in a small room with no whiteboard or flip-chart is nonsensical. If you want to have a short meeting, don't provide chairs—stand-up meetings are easy to keep short. If you want people to participate fully in a brainstorming or problem-solving exercise, make sure the environment is comfortable. Book the meeting room with the comfy chairs, or take everyone out to the nearest coffee shop. Think about whether providing food, coffee, and so on, would be a smart move.

**Keep it short.**

There are very few real situations where a meeting should take longer than one hour, let alone three or four! Usually, long meetings like these are amalgamations of smaller meetings, but someone has been too lazy to break them out into their component parts. Rather than thinking, "How do I get—and keep—everyone in the room?" ask yourself, "What's the smallest group that could discuss this issue and make the right decision?"

**Use a "parking lot."**

Have a flip-chart, whiteboard, or (if you are teleconferencing) a suitably labeled document that can act as your "parking lot." Whenever anyone starts getting into a very detailed discussion that would be better dealt with outside the meeting, "park" it by noting it on the parking lot page. Of course, as the project manager, you'll need to make sure that these issues *are* dealt with, otherwise, you'll just be seen as trying to silence discussion.

## Project Status Updates

Keeping everyone—from the project board, to interested stakeholders—informed of the project's status is important. A best-practice approach to doing this is to send out project status updates either electronically (via email or as a document attached to email) or on paper.

In some organizations, you might even want to hold a regular update mini-meeting, although you should be very careful about doing this unless you're certain it will be appreciated by participants. You don't want to create another pointless meeting that people will only resent!

 **Predictability Is Key**

It's important that stakeholders know when they can expect an update. Updates should be regular and always delivered to the same schedule, if possible—for example, a weekly update sent every Thursday. It's also good to be clear about the process of exceptions. If the Thursday is a public holiday, for instance, should the stakeholders expect an update a day earlier, or the first working day after the original update time?

The typical format of a project status update is as follows:

**high-level status**

The project's high-level status is typically indicated by a combination of description and traffic-light coding: on track (green), some issues (yellow) or off track (red).

**summary of current achievements and issues**

This paragraph describes the current state of the project.

**more detail**

This section's makeup will depend on the nature of your project. You might include the highest level project plan you have, showing the different phases and whether they're on track or not. Alternatively, you might want to list the key issues that require attention, so that the Project Board can understand what you're struggling with.

**attachments**

Common attachments include the current project plan, an issues list, and the original Project Initiation Document, to remind everyone of the original reasons for undertaking the project.

## Plans

As you might expect, your project plan is a key element of your communication and collaboration. All the people in the team (and some stakeholders outside of it) will need to know what will be worked on next, what the key priorities are, and how the work will be distributed.

You can reduce work for yourself and increase the likelihood that your project plan will be kept up to date if you use it as a way of communicating work allocation. You can add people's names to indicate who owns a particular deliverable, and add color-coding to impart status information.

 **Think Before You Send!**

Don't ever just blindly send out your current project plan to anyone who asks about the project. First, think about whether it's the best way to communicate with them. Does it have the right level of detail? Does it contain the information they need? Consider creating a cut-down version if that's needed, rather than swamping people with too much detail.

## Issue Tracking Software

As soon as you encounter more than one or two issues with a project, the value of establishing a central list where issues can be logged, prioritized, and resolutions recorded becomes apparent. A number of different software options are available, some of them open source and free, others incurring the sort of cost that requires senior management approval.

As always, the point is to find the simplest thing that works. For some teams, issue tracking is as simple as a spreadsheet in a shared space; for others it's a tie-in to full-blown project management software. To successfully choose an approach to issue tracking, you'll need to work out which tool will actually be used, and what issue tracking process will be followed *before* you actually encounter any issues. It's easier to educate your team about a process when they aren't worrying about how to fix a specific problem.

 **Reduce the Issue Tracking Burden**

> You may be tempted to ask the team to track all sorts of extra data simply to make your life easier. For instance, you might ask them to track exactly how long it takes to resolve each issue, document exactly what was done to resolve the issue, and whether it worked. All too soon, the issue tracking process will become cumbersome, and people will stop following it. If they feel like they're spending more time tracking issues than they are fixing them, they'll look to circumvent the process. Stick with something simple and effective, and it's much more likely that it will be used.

The main value of issue tracking tools is that they let you see the current state of affairs in one place. You can then easily prioritize the issues that need to be addressed most urgently, and put others on hold (or even decide not to invest effort in resolving them). Sometimes, issues are put on hold when it's realized that a project activity might resolve them. I once worked on a project in which a number of issues were discovered as we worked to automate a process. But all of the issues were placed on hold because we realized that instead of dealing with the issues individually, a completely different tack was needed to achieve the project itself. We completely eliminated the process that was being automated, and achieved the business goal in a different way, so the issues eventually moved from "on hold" status to "will not fix" status.

An issue tracking system will also help you to consider assigning the ownership of different issues to people within the team, and redistributing the workload, for example, when it becomes apparent that one person is having to deal with ten times as many issues as anyone else.

Identifying and categorizing the root cause of issues is not always useful during the project, but it's invaluable when you're looking back on what you've done. For instance, if 80% of your issues in a project were the result of design misunderstandings, there's probably something you can do to change the design process in future. You might not be able to eliminate all the issues, but you could certainly identify them earlier on, when making a change would be cheaper, or preempting them before they become problems.

## Wikis

**Wikis** (web sites to which anyone can add new or edit existing content) can also be useful for issue tracking, but their true value lies in knowledge management. If you have a team that's collaborating on the development of a new software system, for example, using a wiki to collate the rough technical documentation provided by multiple team members can work very effectively.

 **Outgrowing Your Wiki**

The wiki's organic growth potential, and it's ability to be updated easily, combine to form a double-edged sword. When wikis are being actively used and maintained, and are focused on a specific topic or set of topics, they work well. However, as soon as the amount of information that's being recorded grows beyond a certain point, or becomes very diverse, problems arise. At that point, you either need to invest time to add structure, prune and reintroduce content to the right sections, or move to a tool that has an inherent structure.

It may be worth agreeing some sort of structure up-front, but the beauty of wikis is that they evolve, growing organically as new information is added. As with any software solution, you need to make sure that the wiki actually meets the team's needs, and that your team is comfortable using it. Mandating a new tool without providing any support is almost always a waste of time and, potentially, money.

## The RASCI Matrix

**RASCI** is a collaboration matrix that defines different roles that people in the project can play, either for the entire project, or for individual tasks. RASCI goes beyond communication to define the involvement of individuals in deliverables and work. When you have lots of people involved in a project, or stakeholders trying to get more involved than you'd like them to be, RASCI provides clarity and can help you to explain why someone's involvement is (or isn't!) needed.

RASCI is an acronym that can be explained as follows:

**responsible**    The person who's responsible for delivering the piece of work (usually a project deliverable) is the first person to identify. For any given task, only one person should be responsible.

**accountable**    This person is "on the hook"—he or she must make sure the deliverables are completed. In a project situation, the accountable person will almost always be the project manager. You'll approve the deliverable, checking that it meets the appropriate standard, and that it won't damage any other aspect of the product or project.

**supportive**    Supportive parties are people who can help support the person who's responsible, usually by providing help or resources.

**consulted**    The consulted people are those who have information that might be needed, be it data, past experience, or skills. They will typically be consulted in order to deliver the work.

**informed**    These are people who don't need to be involved with, or to approve the work, but would like to know what has been done.

To illustrate how the concept of RASCI can be used in practice, take a look at the snippet I've reproduced from a project RASCI chart in Figure 4.3.

## RASCI Chart - Pie Shop Web Site Project

| Deliverable | Responsible | Accountable | Supportive | Consulted | Informed |
|---|---|---|---|---|---|
| Web site design | Natalie | Meri | Timo, Laura | Saul | Fadil, Laurence |
| CSS framework | Saul | Meri | Natalie | Laurence, Fadil | |
| Shopping cart functionality | Laurence | Meri | Fadil | Saul, Natalie | Timo |

Figure 4.3. An example RASCI matrix

In this example, the project involves creating a web site for a pie shop. The lead designer is Natalie, who's responsible for delivering the web site design. The project manager is Meri, who's ultimately accountable for making sure the deliverables are up to scratch.

Timo and Laura are the marketing folks involved in the project; they playing a supportive role were the web site design is concerned, using their experience of marketing the pie shop to help Natalie understand what the key branding messages will be.

Saul is the main web developer in your team, and he needs to be consulted about what's feasible in terms of design. Fadil and Laurence are going to be building the back end of the web site, where the pages that users see connect to a database. They don't feel like they need to have a say in the design process itself, but as it will affect the work they'll be doing, they'd like to stay Informed.

For any given task or deliverable, the RASCI concept is applied to work out who should be involved in the process, and in what capacity. It's essentially just a very specific way of detailing roles and responsibilities for a set of deliverables.

The crucial point to note is when you use the RASCI matrix, you must ensure that it's developed collaboratively. Those involved need to agree on which role they will be fulfilling—you can't just write up the matrix, email it out, and expect everyone to fall into line!

| Deliverable | Laura | Laurence | Meri | Natalie | Saul | Fadil | Timo |
|---|---|---|---|---|---|---|---|
| Web site design | S | I | A | R | C | I | S |
| CSS framework | | C | A | S | R | C | |
| Shopping cart functionality | | R | A | C | C | S | I |

Figure 4.4. An alternative representation of the RASCI matrix

## Managing Multiple Projects

One of the happy side effects of having created all the project documents, from project plan to issue lists, is that they make managing multiple projects much easier. It is almost a luxury these days to only work on one project at a time—many of us find ourselves juggling a number of projects, and the people on our teams are assigned to many different projects, too.

This can cause complications: team members who don't have 100% of their time assigned to your projects can find themselves torn between the priorities of completely different pieces of work. You may also find it difficult to keep track of all the details of your different projects if you try to keep them all in your head.

Using the project tools makes it easier for you, as well as your team. Emails that are very clear about responsibilities and deadlines help team members to prioritize their work. Status updates help the stakeholders to know what's going on, but they also provide a helpful refresher on the project's current status when you're switching between projects on a daily basis. Issue lists help to ensure that barriers are broken down, and that issues aren't forgotten. Plans help to direct work.

You may even find that you want to expand some of the tools to cover multiple projects—status update newsletters that contain details of all the projects being worked on might be beneficial if the stakeholder group is roughly the same for all the projects. Beware, however, of overintegrating: it may be useful to *you* to have one plan for all the projects, but unless the teams are the same for each project, it may simply confuse everyone else.

# Managing Change

In projects, change is as much a certainty as death and taxes are in life. Dealing with change not only pragmatically but positively is one of the hallmarks of a great project manager. In order to do so, you need to be able to understand the different types of change and reasons for change; to communicate the impact of change effectively so that the right decision can be made and lastly to effectively implement change as necessary.

## Types of Change

There are a number of different reasons why change might be required, but for all those reasons, there are essentially just two types of change:

1. **change arising from a new requirement**

    Some change arises from a new need that is discovered during the course of the project. Usually this occurs because of a change either in internal circumstances (something within the organization or project) or external circumstances (something in the wider world, be it government, legal requirements, or similar).

## 2. change arising from an undocumented requirement

This type of change occurs when an existing need that was somehow overlooked, deemed to be out of scope, or otherwise remained unaddressed, is identified as being a necessary part of the project scope.

For instance, when the Enron scandal hit in the US and the new SOX (Sarbanes Oxley) requirements were introduced, any financial projects running at the time suddenly had a new set of requirements to deal with. SOX not only impacts how the accounting itself is done, it also affects the processes within the company. Technical systems projects would have felt a similar impact when the Y2K problem came to the fore.

Of course, new requirements might be much more mundane than these examples. If you were developing a reporting system for a business that experienced a reorganization, the reporting areas would change because of the reshuffle. Obviously, continuing with the old structure isn't going to make sense, because people aren't working like that anymore, so the change is necessary and unpredicted.

Undocumented requirements can often cause change—consider the cake shop web site project we mentioned in Chapter 3. The client on that project might presume that your team would create the content for the web site as well as completing the technical work to set it up. If this expectation was overlooked in the listing of assumptions during the Planning phase, it could well become a change that will be requested at some point during execution.

It's important to understand which type of change you're dealing with, because the type of change is very likely to affect the perception of how that change should be dealt with. If the project board and your stakeholders feel that you overlooked an obvious requirement (that is, the change is an undocumented requirement), they probably won't take kindly to your suggesting that extra funding is needed to accommodate this need.

Before we get ahead of ourselves and talk about money, however, we need to talk about dealing with requests for change and how to decide whether changes will be made or not.

# Change Control

**Change control** involves having a process for collecting requests for change, investigating the impact of each change, prioritizing those impacts, and getting approval to make a change (given its impact).

First, let's take a step back. I'm sure you're thinking, "Why do we need such a big process for something as simple as making a change? Surely we just do what the customer asks?"

In a perfect world of unlimited time, funding, and resources, you'd be right. We'd take the list of potential changes and just work through them, one by one. But I'm sure that you can think back to a time when "just a few small adjustments" snowballed into days and weeks more work for you or your team—even though that work was never really part of the plan? You'd make the requested change and then something else would need to be changed as well, until eventually the end product was so different from the original design that it was unrecognizable.

Your role as project manager is about making the project happen on time and within budget, and delivering the agreed scope and quality. Part of the point of having you there is to make sure that the project doesn't cost more than it delivers—that there's an acceptable return on investment. No one wants to spend $100,000 on a project that's only worth $50,000.

Change control, then, is really a process of ensuring that the impact of a change is really considered before you go ahead and do it. As with the issue tracking process, it's important to define how changes will be registered and considered up-front, so that when the first changes come along everyone knows how they'll be dealt with.

## The Change Control Process

Though your change control process may be heavily tailored to your environment and project, there are a number of key steps that will apply in all circumstances:

**Gather the change requests (CRs).**
    You want to have some basic information on each requested change, including the benefits it will generate and which parts of the project it affects.

**Understand the impacts.**

Your first step, on receiving a change request, is to form an understanding of the change and what it's going to mean for the project. Will it mean a design change? More work? Less work? Will you need to get a specialist in to make the change, or could your team handle it?

**Communicate the impacts and get a decision.**

Make sure that the project board understands what the change means for the project in terms of cost, time, scope, and quality. At the end of the day, the final decision rests with the board—your role is to make sure they have the appropriate understanding to make the right call. There should only be three possible decisions: yes, make the change; no, don't make the change; and investigate the change further.

### Does the Change Fit the Project?

When you're communicating the impact of a change, make sure you inform the board about the cost, time, quality, and scope impacts of the change. Also refer them to the original reasons why the project was undertaken, and have them consider the question, "Does this change help drive those original needs?"

**Communicate the decision.**

Whether the change is going to be undertaken or not, you need to make sure that you let the stakeholder who proposed it (and any others affected by it) know what the outcome of the review process was. Be careful not to fall into the position of justifying the decision—if the requesters want to argue with the decision, they need to argue with the project board, not you!

**Execute the change.**

If the decision was to go ahead with the change, then you'll need to adjust your plans accordingly, and execute the change. As with the rest of the project, you'll need to ensure that you have control mechanisms in place. That way, if implementing the change turns out to have greater impact than anyone anticipated, you can spot it early and escalate the issue to the board if needed.

Whether you choose to execute the change control process on paper or in electronic format is up to you—consider in particular the nature of the organization you're working with. Personally, I believe that project managers should work to make change control as easy as possible. However, some project managers actively discourage changes by making the change control process arduous—for instance, using paper forms that have to be filled out in triplicate before they will be considered.

Viewing change as the enemy is not a constructive approach. Some changes will indeed mean more work, but stakeholders might also identify real opportunities that'll make a big difference to your project's effectiveness. Involving the project board to make the decision based on the potential value of individual change requests will hopefully weed out the **gold-plating** requests—those that are nice to have, but not essential—leaving only those that make a real difference.

 **Blind Divergence Is Always a Mistake**

Sticking rigidly to the project plan can sometimes be a mistake, but blindly diverging from it without considering the implications of change is *always* a mistake.

## Change Request or Project Deliverable?

One of the most difficult situations you will have to deal with as a project manager arises when stakeholders (and maybe even the project board) feel that something you see as a change was implicit in the original scope of the project.

This leaves you in a very difficult position—you have agreed to a certain scope, and expanding that will have obvious cost and time implications. Your customers, on the other hand, evidently thought it was in your original quote, so they're quite appalled that you want to discuss additional resources or time to make it happen!

It's at times like this that your diligence in the Initiating and Planning phases of the project will really pay off. Revisit the Project Initiation Document and the project plan. Was the deliverable actually identified there, but you've somehow overlooked it? Try to understand why the customer's perceptions differ so much from yours on this point.

If you find that the deliverable *wasn't* included in the original scope, you have two options. You can agree that it was implicit in the scope, and agree to complete the change without additional resources or time. Alternatively, you can point to the scope that was signed off by the board, show that the deliverable in question was not included, and negotiate more resources or time, depending on what's needed.

Of course, there are times when playing hardball on these issues doesn't seem the right thing to do in terms of preserving your relationship with the customer. You may well decide to take a short-term hit to build the long-term relationship. If you choose to take this approach, however, take the opportunity to revisit the project scope—if you've already found one hidden assumption, there may well be others. Don't get stung by the impact of misperceptions—or miscommunications—over and over again. Get everything out in the open, and work out whether you need a full renegotiation of the project if you discover that the customer was expecting the project to include lots of extras that you haven't planned.

# Tools and Best Practices

The change control process can be assisted by the use of several tools.

## The Balance Quadrant

Sometimes it's best to try and illustrate the impact of a change visually. Although we've already talked about the four key areas in the quadrant being time, cost, quality, and scope, it can be very powerful to place these four aspects in a grid and illustrate what the impact of each change will be.

For example, in communicating the impact of a change to add new functionality to a web site that you were building, you could present the two scenarios illustrated in Figure 4.5.

What this diagram indicates is that, whichever path is chosen, it'll entail additional cost and an increase to the project scope. You need the board to choose between is a two-week delay on the project's launch, and a higher instance of bugs if you launch on time, but have had to divert resources to work on the extra functionality.

## Stakeholder Reviews

Encouraging change may seem a strange thing for a project manager to do. After all, change seems to result in all these difficult discussions and decisions, right? While that's true, ensuring that change takes place at the right time can be very powerful.

| Cost | Time | Cost | Time |
|---|---|---|---|
| **Extra $10,000** | **Additional 2 Weeks** | **Extra $10,000** | No Change |
| **Additional Functionality** | No Change | **Additional Functionality** | **Go live with 50% more bugs** |
| Scope | Quality | Scope | Quality |

Figure 4.5. Illustrating the impacts of proposed changes with the balance quadrant

Stakeholder reviews provide a means for inviting input and anticipating potential change early in the process, when changes will likely be less expensive to make.

The later you leave change, the more expensive it will be. It's almost always more difficult and more costly to change something that has already been built than it is to change the design before a single brick (be it literal or figurative) is laid.

This point is obvious in projects that produce something physical. Everyone understands that asking for the windows in the house you're building to be moved six inches higher after the walls have been built will be expensive. Making that change while the design is still on paper is straightforward and cheap; making it later in the process means breaking down bricks that have already been laid. Illustrating this point is a simple matter of walking around on site.

The problem in knowledge work is that the detail of what needs to be reworked, knocked down, or rebuilt is more difficult to explain. The deliverables seem more ethereal, so stakeholders may misunderstand their impacts. For instance, if you've designed your database system with the storage of text files in mind, a sudden change of requirements that means you need to accommodate audiovisual content will have a big impact on this aspect of the project.

Involving stakeholders early, so that they can highlight missing pieces of the puzzle, or communicate their bright ideas for improvement is a smart way of getting ahead of the curve. Manage change or it will manage you!

So what does a stakeholder review actually involve? Essentially, it's just a matter of meeting with stakeholders and reviewing the project plans with them. If you're building a product, you might show them the early design sketches or prototypes.

In the technology realm, this kind of user involvement is best practice in any case—many aspects of the interaction design, usability testing, and user-centered design processes rely on the product's early exposure to users.

Be careful, though, that you don't go too far. The point of stakeholder reviews is to gain input, not to try to have your stakeholders and users actually design the product themselves.

## Change Requests

Change requests (CRs) can take many forms—you may be happy to accept CRs via email, provided the required information is provided in each one. You might want people to fill in an electronic form, or summarize what they want in a Word document. The important point is to garner sufficient information quickly, so that you can evaluate the scope and impact of the change.

Typically, the a change request involves these sections:

**proposer**          the details of the person who's requesting the change, including his or her contact details

**description**       an explanation of the change that's being requested

**business benefit**  a description of the value the change will deliver, and how it will be delivered

**priority**          an identification of the importance of the change requested

There should also be a section either on the change request form itself, or in the tracking system you're using, to collate the CRs together, enabling you and your team members to add in information about the impacts of the change—effectively answering questions such as, What would be involved? How much would it cost? And how long would it take?

## Change Review Boards

If you don't receive many change requests, you might just add an agenda point to your regular project board meetings to discuss the proposed changes. However, if you're getting a large number of CRs to consider, or you need to have a decision on a CR before the next project board meeting, you might want to call a change review board—a meeting that will allow you to consider the different CRs and make decisions about which to proceed with.

If a number of different CRs are vying for resources, it may be smart to invite stakeholder advocates to come to the board and "make their cases" for the changes they requested. Much as you're giving the project board the hard facts (including the time, cost, impacts on scope and quality), organizational considerations that you're not well placed to comment on may also come into play. In such cases, bring in one advocate for each change request, and give him or her a few minutes to present the case for that change.

This kind of approach can have a number of positive effects:

- The project board receives extra information that can help them make the best decisions for the project.

- The stakeholders get to see the value of the other change requests that have been submitted. They may realize that other needs should take priority for the good of the project, and the organization.

- Some stakeholders may find that they will benefit from changes proposed by another area—changes that may possibly even negate the need for their own change request to be acted upon.

In this kind of meeting, your role is largely that of coordinator. You want everyone to get a fair hearing, and for decisions to be made at the end of the meeting. Try to keep people focused on the value of the changes by asking direct questions about the value that each change will deliver, and trying to defuse any overly emotional reactions.

## Replanning Sessions

The outcome of many change requests is an agreement to go ahead and make the change. If a number of CRs have been considered and approved, a larger replan may be needed than if just one or two changes have been given the go-ahead—though of course, that will depend on the nature of the approved changes! Either way, the approval of changes provides a good opportunity to bring your team together for a replanning and brainstorming session.

As in previous planning rounds, involving the team will really help them to feel a sense of ownership for the deliverables they'll be working on. It's also a great chance to find opportunities to work smarter rather than harder.

For instance, if a number of the changes that have just been agreed are going to affect the same aspect of the product, making the design changes for them all together will likely be a sensible approach. You might even find some overlaps which actually mean that the total impact of all the changes is less than the sum of the individual impacts!

# Summary

We started this chapter by considering communication and why it's so important to successful project management. We discussed the forms (one-to-one, one-to-many, many-to-many), methods (email, face-to-face meetings, instant messenger, and so on), and contents (purpose, structure, and outcomes) of communication, as well as the different preferences that people have for the aspects of communication.

We then talked about collaboration, and saw how you can take a group of individuals and turn it into a team that works. We talked about the process of team formation, which involves the steps of forming, storming, norming, performing, and adjourning (or mourning). We talked about the difference between management and leadership, and saw that, as people have different levels of ability and motivation for tasks, you need to alter your management style accordingly.

We then explored a range of tools and best practices that can help you to communicate and collaborate effectively, including rules for email etiquette, meeting standards, project status updates, plans, issue tracking software, wikis, and the RASCI matrix.

The second part of this chapter addressed the issues associated with managing change. A defined change control process is essential to the success of any project, ans it allows you to ensure that change requests are collected, the impact of the proposed changes are considered, and a measured decision is made about each.

The tools and best practices that we discussed in relation to change control included the balance quadrant. stakeholder reviews, change requests, change review boards, and replanning sessions.

Now that we've discussed communication, collaboration, and handling change, it's time to set our sights on the home stretch: closing the project and moving on to other endeavours.

Chapter

# 5

## Following Through

At this point, you're familiar with most of the project life cycle. You've successfully initiated your project and been through a number of loops of the Planning, Executing, and Controlling phases. You've understood the business value of the project, and have driven towards this at every decision point in the project. You've kept stake-holders, your project board, and, of course, your team informed and involved. Most of all, you've managed change well, and now you're approaching the finish line.

In this chapter, we'll talk about the final phase of the project life cycle: Closing. We'll also discuss what comes next, whether it's handing the project over to another team, or running the day-to-day operations of the finished product yourself. Finally, we'll consider how to move on to new projects without your customers feeling like you've deserted them!

## Closing the Project

In order to complete the final phase of the project life cycle—Closing—we first need to talk about how we know we're ready for it. How do we know when a project is finished? And what will we do if the customer doesn't agree that we're done? Once we've considered this all-important point, we'll talk about the actual process of closing the project. We'll also consider some useful tools and best practices that will help you to close out smoothly and effectively.

## Knowing When You're Done

Knowing when you are ready to move out of the Planning, Controlling, and Executing cycle, and on to closing the project seems deceptively simple. You just move on to closing once you've finished the actual *doing* of the project, right?

Well ... maybe. On closer inspection, identifying the end of the project isn't so simple. Do you draw the line when most of the project deliverables have been completed? When people on your team are starting to run out of work and you need to release them? When the business value promised has been delivered?

There are compelling reasons to close at any of these points. Once the majority of project deliverables have been completed, your project team will start to run out of things to do. No one wants to waste resources, and although folks in the team might find it a welcome relief to have a couple of days with less to do, having no work for an extended period of time is boring. Realistically, their skills are probably in high demand—in some cases you may find you have to fight to keep your team together right up until the end of the project!

On the other hand, the business value promised may take a while to be delivered—after all, many projects focus on delivering a product or designing a new process that will deliver results in the longer term. In contrast, your project's focus will have been on creating that product or process and making sure it's adopted. Obviously, you wouldn't want to keep resources tied up until that value was delivered.

Knowing the right time to close can be tricky, but if you did your initiating right, you'll know exactly when you're approaching the home stretch.

Back when we initiated the project, we wrote and agreed on a Project Initiation Document. Along with some basic details of scope, time lines, and so on, it also included a section that defined success criteria.

These success criteria describe what you're trying to achieve in the project itself, as well as the long-term business benefits that are expected as the pay back for the initial investment in the project. One of the reasons that keeping the PID up to date as the project progresses, and changes are made to its scope, time, quality, and cost factors, is to make sure that these success criteria are still relevant.

The time to start thinking about closing the project is when the currently agreed set of success criteria will soon be met.

How far in advance you will realize you're about to hit your success criteria and start working on the Closing phase will depend on the overall length of your project. On a three-week project, you might only realize it a couple of days in advance. On a three-year project, you'll probably realize that you're heading towards completion two to three months in advance.

 **Don't Fixate on "The Date"**

If you've been very focused on a particular date—whether it's a key date on which a new process will begin to be used, or a product will be launched—you might fall into the trap of thinking that this is the end of the project. It's important to draw the distinction between key dates and the actual end of the project.

For instance, in the run-up to the end of 1999, many technology companies and IT departments were very focused on January 1, 2000, since that was when the Y2K risk was expected to take effect. Y2K projects needed to have all relevant code changes completed by this date, but the projects themselves would probably not have been closed until sometime in the year 2000. Activities that might have occurred after the key date would have included documentation, extra support in case new bugs were introduced in the rush to fix date issues, and the actual process of closing the project and celebrating its success (or investigating its failure!).

## Gaining Customer Agreement

You cannot decide independently, as project manager, that a project can be closed. As in every other part of your project, the team, the project board, and your stakeholders will have their own opinions on the topic, and these will need to be taken into account. To put it bluntly, at the end of the day, your customer is the only fat lady who can sing!

In reality, there are three scenarios:

### 1. total success

The project has delivered everything that was planned, it all works perfectly, and you've become such a hero that they're building a statue in your honor. People in the office high-five you as you walk past. In a movie, you'd be the character with whom the perky theme tune was always associated.

### 2. compromise

The project has delivered the most important elements, and through a review of the project success criteria, you and the customer will come to an agreement that the project can be closed. It's likely there are a number of conditions that need to be met before they will be 100% happy.

### 3. total disconnect

You (and probably your team members) believe that you've done what you were asked to do, but the customers are in a completely different place. They either think you've broken your contract with them, or they didn't realize the implications of what they agreed to at the outset, so they're continually moving the finish line.

It will probably come as no surprise to you that scenarios two and three are more likely than scenario one. Every now and again you'll get the awesome feeling of having totally hit one out of the park, but usually you'll be aiming for compromise and consensus. After all, complex projects have complex results. What you need to avoid is the total disconnect.

A good project manager should be able to do this by keeping customers (both the stakeholders and the project board) engaged and involved through the project. As always, it's not a problem if people to disagree with you, but it will be a big deal if that disagreement, distrust, and unhappiness comes at you around a blind corner.

Hopefully, you have the finger on the pulse, so you know what the customer reaction is going to be when you start talking about closing the project. If you're faced with a situation of total disconnect, the next section is for you—it explains how to deal with this scenario. However, if you're faced with either of the other scenarios, you can begin the process of closing the project.

# Handling a Total Disconnect

Somewhere in the past of every seasoned project manager there's The Project That Went Wrong. We all learn by making mistakes, and it's fairly safe to say that we've all found ourselves in the awful total disconnect situation, convinced that we're in the right and that our team has done what it was asked to do, and totally bewildered by the fact that the customers seem to have turned into angry, bitter, screaming monsters at the mere suggestion that the project is almost finished.

If you find yourself in this situation, you need to go into what I like to call "emergency mode." The first thing you *must* do is **stop**. Stop talking about closing the project, stop talking about moving your people on to other projects or client accounts, and most of all, stop trying to convince your customers that you've done what they asked you to. Though all of these may seem like sensible actions, in fact they're just going to inflame the situation further and infuriate your project's customers.

The second thing you need to do is **listen**. Don't sit there looking bored and thinking of your next comeback while they rant: really *listen*. Don't talk other than to ask clarifying questions. Let your customers rant, vent, let it all out. You need to understand what's really wrong, how the disconnect arose, and how it developed without you realizing it. When they stop, ask "Is there anything else?" Sometimes you'll need to talk through multiple layers of anger and frustration before you reach the fundamental problem.

Next, you need to **understand**. You may need to talk to multiple people before you really understand what the issue is, so don't rush into it. Once you've listened to someone, repeat their key points to ensure you've understood their concerns, but don't suggest solutions or start bargaining. Just make sure you comprehend what they're saying, then go and talk to the other people whose points of view you need to understand. Keep doing this even when you feel bruised and battered from all the negativity. It's important that you really understand what the problem is.

By this point you'll have achieved two very important goals. First, you'll have formed a true understanding of what's gone wrong, and an appreciation for your customers' points of view. Second, you'll have taken a lot of the emotion out of the situation. Really listening to your customers will remove a lot of the anger, hurt, and frustration they're feeling. And calm people are a lot easier to bargain with.

The next thing you'll need to do is to **form solutions**—work out paths that will take you forward. In all likelihood, you'll have shielded your project team from the wrath of the customers, but team members need to understand the issue so that they can help you come up with ways to solve it. So share the customers' issues with them, and brainstorm a range of solutions.

In most cases, your options are likely to look something like this:

- Scrap the project and start over.
- Close this project and start a new one to address the gaps.
- Renegotiate your definition of success, and formulate a new plan to achieve it.

Of course, the usual time, cost, scope, and quality implications will need to be considered. It's usually at this point that things become sticky, because the question of who will bear the cost (monetary or otherwise) of the chosen solution is likely to be hotly contested. If you're an outside contractor, this might be a good time to consult your lawyer and check the exact terms and conditions of your contract. If you're an internal project manager delivering a project for a department other than your own, you probably want to get your managers involved at this point to help negotiate.

The next step is to **renegotiate**. Present your potential solutions to the project board and ask the board members to decide which route should be taken. Be honest about the implications of each option; give the board the data it needs to make the best decision.

If part of the reason you wound up in this mess is that you didn't have a project board, this is the time to form one. In crisis situations, it's important to have the right people make the decisions. You needn't call the group a project board, of course—they can be an emergency committee, a customer review panel, or whatever. The name's not important. What's important is that you have the people with both the ability and the authority making the big decisions.

Once a decision has been reached, you can **continue**. Form the new plan, kick off the new project, close the existing project—take whatever steps have been agreed. Whatever you do, make sure that you don't start again until you're confident that the new approach will have a better outcome than the old one.

# Closing a Project

Closing your project involves a four step process: review, agree, complete, and celebrate. As in other project activities, it's important, first of all, to determine who needs to be involved in each step. For instance, you might want to celebrate the project being completed with everyone involved, but actually completing the final tasks would primarily involve your project team.

Let's take a closer look at each of these phases now.

## Review

The first step in closing is to review the project, presenting the product or process that has been delivered. Your focus should be on the success criteria that were agreed in the Initiating phase, and were revisited regularly when changes were made during the Planning, Executing, and Controlling phases. Consider each success criterion, and show either how it has been achieved, or why it won't be achieved.

If a decision has been taken not to try and achieve a given success criterion (for whatever reason), it may be worth reminding the audience about when that decision was taken and why. Significant decisions like these would normally have been taken by the project board. For instance, the project may have required that one of the ISO quality standards was met, but the associated cost of producing all the documentation may have been deemed excessive, so this success criterion may have been amended or removed during the course of the project.

You should also give an overview of the starting point for the project (the original Project Initiation Document is a good tool here) and highlight the changes that were made to the four areas of the balance quadrant: key decisions that impacted cost, time, quality, and scope.

Your project review (which will typically be a meeting, as we'll discuss below) should essentially answer four questions:

1. Has the project come in on or under budget?
2. Has the project been delivered on time?
3. Has the project delivered the required scope?
4. Has the project been delivered to the required standard of quality?

**What *Not* to Do In Your Project Review**

**Don't show a live demo.**

If you've built a product, and you want to demonstrate it, set up a demo that's separate from the project review. You don't want people to focus on the detail of the product while you're trying to close the project itself. In any case, it's best to share the demonstrations as soon as possible, to show progress in your project, rather than waiting until the end!

**Don't discuss the details of any changes.**

Don't get into the detail of why certain changes were or weren't included. This is not the time for stakeholders to dispute change approvals or disapprovals made by the project board (or change board).

**Don't revise the project's history.**

Your project review is about reviewing the project, not making yourself or your team look good. Don't start rewriting the course of events—people in the audience will notice, and you'll lose credibility while derailing your meeting. Focus on what was achieved, and steer clear of trying to make excuses.

## Agree

The next step is to gain agreement on exactly what remains to be done before the project can be officially closed. You'll probably already have put some thought into this as part of your project planning, but since customer agreement is such a key part of the Closing phase, it's important for this stage to be very transparent for everyone involved. Typical deliverables at this stage would be documentation, training for those who will perform the new process or support the product, and administrative tasks such as completing final budget reconciliations.

If, in your project review meeting, there's literally nothing else to be done on the project, you've probably left the review too late. If there's nothing left to do, your project team has probably been sitting idle. It's better to have the review meeting as the finish line is approached, and agree how to take the last few steps together, than to have everyone hanging around twiddling their thumbs.

## Complete

The next stage is to complete the final tasks and deliverables that were agreed to. How well you execute this point is going to heavily influence people's perceptions of how the project was handled, so it's important to pay attention to detail. Dot the i's and cross the t's, and make sure the documentation is completed properly and training is given due attention.

As your team members are likely to be winding down on this project and may already be starting up on others, it can be easy for them to get distracted. After all, the new project may seem more exciting than writing up documentation or similar, seemingly administrative, tasks.[1] You may find that it's more necessary at this stage than any other to keep a close eye on your progress and to follow up regularly with those who are responsible for delivering these last few milestones.

It's also worth overcommunicating at this stage. The review stage will have brought a spotlight to bear on the project, so make sure that people are kept informed about progress and any delays.

Particularly if you were operating under a formal contract, one of the final tasks should certainly be getting official sign-off from the customer that the project has been delivered. You should also specify any future relationship, whether it be that you will be providing ongoing operational support, or handing over to another team. We'll discuss this further in the next section.

## Celebrate

Last, but certainly not least, it's important to celebrate the end of the project! It's easy for projects to fizzle out as they're completed, for the new process or product to become the status quo for the stakeholders, for the project board's attention to be diverted elsewhere, and for project team members to float off to their next projects or assignments.

The project managers that I most enjoyed working with were those that were brave enough to face reality and generous enough to give credit where it was due. They never gave false praise—when they applauded you for a job well done, you always

---

[1] Incidentally, this is another great reason to make sure that these tasks are dealt with throughout the course of the project, rather than leaving them all to the end!

knew their praise was genuine, which made it all the more valuable. And when they held a project celebration, the focus was always on the team and what it had achieved, not the amount of alcohol consumed or the fanciness of the venue.

Make a concerted effort to celebrate the end of the project and to make sure that everyone knows what was delivered, both in terms of the process or product developed, and the business value delivered. It may be months or even years since the original rationale for doing the project was shared—since then, the project has become an entity all its own.

Though you shouldn't have let the focus become diverted from the value you were creating by undertaking the project, it can be easy for the wider organization to forget. Celebration is a great opportunity to remind everyone why the project was undertaken, and what value it promises, and also to recognize individual contributions from the team members or stakeholders.

## Tools and Best Practices

The selection of tools and best practices that will help you through the closing process are as follows.

### The Project Review Meeting

The review and agree stages of the Closing phase should happen as part of a project review meeting. Typically, this would take place as a presentation to the project board, with key stakeholders also invited to attend and participate. Your team members should also be present, and it may be smart to distribute the presentation among them, so that those who have made particular contributions get to display their work.

The project review meeting should not be a blow-by-blow account of the project, though. The focus needs to remain on the products or processes that have been delivered, and keeping these meetings short and crisp is the best way to make them effective. By the end of the meeting you want two things: firstly, an agreement that the project can be closed, and secondly, a list of the items or tasks that need to be completed before the end of the project. This should be a checklist of the final acceptance criteria for the project.

This is potentially the most important meeting of your entire project. Make sure that you send out an agenda well in advance, and that all the key people are able to attend. Make sure that those who are invited understand how crucial the meeting is (follow up on a one-to-one basis if you feel it's required) and that they understand this is the "speak now or forever hold your peace" moment. Define the outcomes that you want (that is, agreement and next steps) up-front and standards for the meeting (for example, that you won't dive into detail unless it's crucial to achieving the meeting's outcomes). Most of all, try to keep to time, and to keep everyone in the room engaged. A project review in which people pay more attention to their email or Sudoku puzzles than to what is being said is almost a guarantee that **zombie stakeholders**—stakeholders who keep "coming back from the dead" with requests for changes or improvements after the project has been closed—will haunt you in the future.

 **Be Prepared!**

Prepare well for this meeting. You need to have details of the changes that were agreed to and exactly when those decisions were made. Having details of the budget used, projections of whether the final bits of work can be completed on time, and the relevant quality and scope information (such as the percentage of product tests passed, for example) will show that you are in control.

## Project Sign-off

Formal project sign-off is desirable in any project, but it's absolutely essential when you're in a contractual relationship. You should pull together a document that details what was delivered, and references the original Project Initiation Document as well as the change log of decisions made through the project. Ideally, it should very closely mirror the original PID, checking off the deliverables that have been completed. Again, the focus here is on what was delivered and the key decisions that were made, not the minutiae of what happened step by step through the project.

Getting the customer (usually the project sponsor and board) to sign on the dotted line to agree that you have delivered what was asked is good practice for closing the project, but also great insurance against queries and concerns in the future.

We'll talk more in the next section about making arrangements for the future. If you'll be providing ongoing maintenance or even running the day-to-day operations of the project's product, you'll also want to attach and reference details of these arrangements and any associated contracts or service level agreements.

 **Be Prepared**

Formal sign-off can be a crystallizing point. Board members who may have happily agreed in the review meeting that the project can be closed may hesitate to officially give their signature to that fact. Something about signing a piece of paper and the associated perception of legality can make people very cautious. So take extra care to pay attention to the details and get all your facts right, since this is the time they're most likely to be examined and questioned.

## Customer Feedback and a Key Measures Score

Both these tools achieve the same end: they help you obtain feedback from your customers about how the project was run. The focus here is on the project management process itself, rather than what has been delivered.

The customer feedback session or survey is a free-form exercise—you might want to design a few key questions around whether the customer felt appropriately involved, well informed, and so on, but you're mainly trying to get their perspective on how well you ran the project, what you did well, and what you could have done better. In the absence of a more formal framework, this is the best way to gather feedback.

If there are a number of customer representatives (say multiple stakeholders in addition to the project board), you might want to hold a face-to-face session, with the atmosphere of a group brainstorm rather than a formal review. You might feel respondents will communicate more freely if you collect feedback anonymously via an electronic or paper survey.

Either way, the mere act of asking for feedback can leave a very positive impression on your customers—they will appreciate that you care about improving, and want to learn from the experience.

If you're working in or for an organization that has a little more sophistication in its project management operations, you might complete a **key measures score**. This is a series of criteria that are used to define the project's success. The criteria will vary from organization to organization, but typically include measures relating to properly initiating, planning, executing, controlling, and closing your project, as well as appropriate communication and documentation.

As with any test, it's nice to know what the questions will be in advance, so if you work in or with an organization that values key measures scores, be sure to ask about them up-front. It probably won't lead you to run your project any differently, but it might save you some time to know that there's a desire for plans or document-ation to be set out in a particular format or meet certain standards.

Some organizations evaluate key measures via self-assessment—that is, the project team marks itself on the different measures. Others ask the customers to evaluate the project's performance against these measures. A blended approach may also be used. Make sure that you understand the implications of such scores—some com-panies view them as a very important performance measure, and may link compens-ation to the score achieved.

## The Lessons Learned Session

While the tools we've just discussed focus on getting customer feedback on how the project was managed, a lessons learned session is an opportunity for the project team to reflect on what went well, what didn't, and what could be done differently in future.

The focus of this session shouldn't be on assigning blame for things that went wrong in the course of the project, but on learning from experience. The best way to do this tends to be by holding a brainstorm session, potentially using the project plan or status update documents to jog people's memories about what might have happened towards the beginning of the project.

It's important to try and keep the team focused on the positives as much as the negatives—it's easy for the group to zone in on the mistakes that have been made without realizing that there were lots of ideas that worked well and should be re-applied in future. Keeping the right balance ensures that the session doesn't become demotivating.

**Being Consciously Positive**

Personally, I prepare for these sessions by consciously writing down everything positive I can think of, so that during the meeting I can pepper the conversation with encouragement for a job well done if the team starts to focus too much on the problems encountered and mistakes made.

After you've held the brainstorming meeting, it's useful to compile a document summarizing what was discussed, and what lessons were learned through the project. Think of it as a one-page summary of everything you learned about project management on that particular project. When you're kicking off a new project, having a collection of such one-pagers to read through can help you avoid pitfalls and improve your chances of success.

 **Expanding the Audience**

You might also choose to hold a lessons learned review with an audience that's wider than just the project team. Others in your organization might also be able to learn from the tools and best practices you used and found successful, as well as the pitfalls you've identified.

## The Closure Celebration

Once the project is truly completed, the final loose ends tied up, and your documentation, training, and handover are all completed, it's time to celebrate! Hopefully you have achieved some great results by completing this project, and now's your opportunity to recognize everyone's hard work, as well as reminding the organization of the value that's been delivered.

It's easy to forget about this "softer" side of project management, but letting your project team and stakeholders just drift away as the project fizzles out is not a winning strategy. Last impressions count, so take the opportunity to celebrate what's been achieved. It's a rare project that manages to be completed without at least some cause for celebration.

Usually some sort of public gathering is appropriate—depending on the organization you're working for, the local bar or an in-house conference room may be the best venue. Strive to include everyone—and realize that this may mean scheduling the celebration during working hours so that those with family or other commitments aren't excluded.

In addition, you might want to follow up to make sure that members of the team who really did well are recognized for it. Often, you'll have working in your team people who don't report to you directly from a career perspective. Take the time to talk to these team members' managers, put in that promotion recommendation, or even award some sort of prize if you feel that's appropriate.

Making sure that individuals are rewarded for good work has an impact not only on the project you're just finishing, but for future projects as well. If the next person assigned to one of your project teams realizes that hard work will be noticed, you're more likely to get that star performance than if they figure that you can have no impact on their salary, promotion prospects, or anything other than whether they get home on time today.

# What Comes Next?

Projects aren't undertaken in a vacuum, nor does their closure mean that there's nothing else to be done. In order to effectively close your project, you also need to think about what happens next.

In doing so, you first need to consider your own role (or that of the organization you're working for). Are you going to be involved in the ongoing operations of the product, or do you need to hand it over to another group that will run the process or product that your project developed?

Delivering the project on time, within budget, to the required level of quality and scope makes you a good project manager. Making sure that the training and documentation are set up so that the promised value will continue to be delivered into the future makes you an amazing project manager.

## Defining Your Role

Up until this point, your role has been to manage the project—to bring it in on time, within budget, to the required levels of scope and quality. Once this is done, however, you might have a number of different roles.

For instance, you might be in charge of the department that will execute the process your project defined, or use the product that your project built. If this is the case, your focus will shift to ensuring that the process or product can be used as effectively as possible. You will become an operational manager, concerned with the day-to-day running of the business.

Alternatively, you might not be involved at all in the day-to-day operations of your product, but you may still be expected to provide support if something goes wrong with it. For instance, if your project was to deliver some new software to control the manufacturing lines at a pet food factory, you're unlikely to have to manage the orders for horse meat, but you might be expected to come back and arrange the eradication of a bug in the software that was erroneously labeling all the dog food as "PussyDLite."

Of course, in all likelihood, you may have none of these roles—you're quite likely to move off to managing a completely different project, potentially in a different organization, particularly if you operate as a contractor or consultant. However, you need to realize that someone will be operating in these roles, and that you will be judged on how well you equip them to do their jobs post-project. When we discuss tools later in this chapter, we'll discuss best practices for documentation and handover that will make this happen smoothly.

Understanding your role in the future of the project (or the process or product that was developed) is very important as it will help you to prioritize what matters most as you close the project and look to the future.

## Knowing When to Renegotiate

One of the primary reasons for understanding how your role is changing as the project finishes is so that you know when to renegotiate. For instance, it may have become apparent that the customer expects ongoing support and maintenance once the new software system that you have installed is deployed. This may not have been included in your original project contract, in which case, you'd need to renegotiate the relationship and define how this ongoing support service will work.

On the other hand, if you're an internal project manager, there's a real risk that you will move on to other projects, only to find yourself continually pulled back into the fray on projects that you finished long ago. At first it may feel wonderful to be needed, and the comfort zone of the completed project may be a welcome reprieve from the uncertainty and challenges of your current projects.

However, if every time you finish a project a little bit more of your time is going to be taken up maintaining and responding to questions on your old projects, you'll soon find that you don't have enough time to focus on the present! Creating great documentation of the project itself (in the form of the plans, issue lists, change logs, and so on, that you were already maintaining) is a great help in shortcutting the questions. And putting proper structures in place to deal with ongoing support, maintenance, and day-to-day operations is what will set your project up for true, long-term success.

You may indeed be the right person to provide those services, but if this is the case, it needs to be negotiated up-front. Having such expectations evolve over time will only result in you being viewed as a failure on both fronts—first, for never properly handing over the original project, and second, for failing to deliver your new projects properly because you're always looking back.

Whether you're an internal project manager moving on to other projects in the same organization, or a contractor keen to provide services on an ongoing basis, it is important to define your role. It's equally important to lay the ground rules for how that new role will work—be it via a formal contract (definitely a must if you're an external contractor!) or a simple memo or agreement.

## The Superstar Handover

Project handover consists of two aspects: **training** and **documentation**. Training tends not to be a big problem. After all, it's been expected all along that people will need to be trained on how to follow the new process, or use the new product that has been developed.

If you've been forward-thinking, you'll have realized that whoever will be doing support in future will need extra, in-depth, technical training so that they understand not just the *what*, but also the *how* and the *why* of the project.[2] This will allow the

---

[2] In this case, "technical" should be read in a broader sense than simply to mean "relating to technology." For instance, if you were defining a new financial process, the required technical understanding would include an in-depth knowledge of accounting principles and practices.

person tasked with the product's operation to complete that extra level of troubleshooting in case something goes wrong.

On the other hand, excitement levels in your life have to be at an especially low ebb for project documentation to be one of the highlights of your week. It's safe to say that documentation is one of those deliverables that everybody loves to hate.

Sadly, project documentation is a boring task that's really quite essential. Imagine, for instance, that your entire team enters a lottery pool, and they win $20 million the day after the project is completed. Reaching those team members on their private beaches to ask questions about how to get the pet food labeling software to stop printing in hieroglyphics will become very difficult.

This example is definitely extreme, but the underlying issue—namely, that after a very short time no one from the original project team will be available to answer questions or deal with issues—is a very real one. People move on to new roles, leave companies, or move across the country every day. And although some initial teething troubles may mean that support is top of the agenda immediately after a project has gone live, there may well be weeks, months or even years of trouble-free operation before that first Big Question or Big Problem is encountered.

As such, investing in documentation and training is essential. The good news is that throughout the project you've been documenting! The Project Initiation Document, project plan, issue lists, project board meeting minutes, change proposals, and project change log already paint a fairly complete picture of what happened through the project, and who was involved. The project sign-off documents the agreed project outcome.

Pulling together these documents, identifying any gaps, and binding it all together with a brief document should give adequate documentation of the project management side of things.

On the other hand, the documentation of the process or product that was the focus of the project should be one of the project deliverables. In the same way, training should be developed as part of the project itself, not just as an afterthought at the end of the project. We're discussing it here because it's so important for a successful project closing, but in fact the actual work should have been done back in the Planning, Executing, and Controlling loops.

**Documentation Is as Important as Training**

At this point, it pays to work very closely with the people who'll be taking over the operational and support work. Don't fall into the trap of relying too heavily on informal training and handover. Unless your role is officially defined as making sure they are trained so they can produce the documentation (which does occasionally happen), make sure you have the hard copy to back up your soft skills.

Defining how handover of day-to-day operations will work, and what the ongoing support model is, should also have been a project deliverable. Don't worry if you have forgotten these tasks, or left them until the Closing phase. Essentially all you're going to do is a final loop through the PEC cycle in order to complete these deliverables.

# Tools and Best Practices

Let's take a look at the tools and best practices that can help you through the handover process.

## The Project Documentation Pack

We've already alluded to the first weapon in your arsenal here. The project documentation pack consists of all the project artifacts, from the initial Project Initiation Document to the project plans, issue lists, and change logs, and finally the project sign-off.

Slap a table of contents on the front, and reference the documentation, training, and any subsequent contracts or agreements that cover the product's ongoing operations. It pays to deliver this pack not only to the project board, but also to the folks who will be operating the product and providing support in future. If there's some sort of shared document repository, store it there as well.

Finally, keep a copy for your records. That way, even if you're approached with questions, you can simply hand over the bundle of documentation, rather than having to wrack your brains for the details of a project long finished.

## Service Level Agreements

If you're going to be providing ongoing support for the product or process that your project delivered, you need a **service level agreement** (SLA). This defines exactly what support is expected and on what timings it should be delivered. For instance, it would define the different types of events that are supported (incidents, problems, changes), as well as the severity levels that the events may be awarded (critical, major, minor, routine) and the agreed targets for resolving each event type.

As an example, let's imagine you're providing ongoing support for a customer order web site. An example of a critical (highest severity) event—an issue that breaks regular service—might be the web site being completely unavailable. This is both the most severe and the most urgent issue possible, as no orders can be received until the web site is restored. As a result, this kind of severe, urgent issue would need a fast response, probably within a matter of hours.

Of course, not everything needs to be dealt with so quickly. The underlying issues that cause events to occur over and over might only be fixed weeks or months after they're discovered, depending on the severity of the problems they cause. It's important to define the levels of service up-front, since negotiating at a time when your customer is actually experiencing a severe incident is either going to be seen as blackmail, or your lack of ability to prioritize issues!

If you're working in the technology space, a wealth of best practices have been documented around the creation and administration of service level agreements. One of the most widely acknowledged frameworks is ITIL—the Information Technology Infrastructure Library. Check Appendix B for references to further resources.

## Operational Contracts

If you're going to have any ongoing involvement after your project is closed, you need to consider your contractual position. The contract for the project probably didn't mention ongoing support, and even if it did, you'd want to revisit that now. Making sure that everyone is aligned on what's expected up-front is much cheaper than dealing with a law suit later.

When you're drawing up an operational contract, you need to consider the measures that are included very carefully. What you measure will drive the behavior of both your and the client's organizations. We've all been on the phone with a call-centre employee who's evidently being assessed on the length of their calls (the shorter the better!). The person seems more focused on palming you off to another department than actually answering your query or fixing your problem.

This isn't because the person's bad at the job—in fact, he or she is doing exactly what the measurement approach requires. The problem is that the measure isn't well aligned with the actual purpose of the organization—to provide customer service! When you're drawing up operational contracts, take care to ensure that the measures defined are appropriate, measurable, and realistic.

## Summary

This chapter kicked off with a discussion of the final phase of the project cycle: Closing. We explained how we can identify the point at which we should start closing the project, and explored the importance of customer agreement. We also considered how to recover from a total disconnect situation in which you and your customer are of completely different opinions.

We then talked through the actual process of closing, including the need to review, agree, complete, and celebrate. The tools and best practices that were recommended for closing included the project review meeting, project sign-off, customer feedback and key measures score, a lessons learned session, and of course, the closure celebration.

Next, we talked about what comes after the project closure. We saw that you need to begin by working out what your role is. Are you going to run the product's ongoing operations, provide support, or simply move on to another project altogether? Whatever your ongoing role will be, excellent handover is extremely important—that's why we talked about how best to achieve it. The tools we discussed—the project documentation pack, service level agreements, and operational contracts—will, without doubt, help smooth the handover process.

Now, we've completed a project, let's talk about your future as a project manager!

## Looking to the Future

Now that you have successfully closed your project, taking care to ensure that it was appropriately documented, and that handover was successful, you need to look to the future. In many cases, this will mean a new project and a new beginning. And in some cases, it might mean a follow-up project that delves into detail on a new issue or opportunity that was discovered in your last project.

Whatever the content of your next project, it will present an opportunity to further hone your skills as a project manager, and your mastery of the project management toolbox.

# The Next Project ... and the Rest

The beauty of project management is that the toolkit remains the same, no matter what project you're undertaking. The science of project management lies in understanding the processes, tools, and best practices that are associated with the job. The art of project management is all about developing the judgment, intuition, and soft skills to choose the right tools, people, and processes, and the finesse to use them to great effect.

As your experience increases, you'll become more confident about choosing the right tool for each aspect of a project. You may also find that, as you work on bigger and more complex projects, more rigor—and more advanced tools—are required. Appendix B provides pointers to some resources that will give you these advanced skills, while Appendix C is designed to help you explore the option to pursue professional project management qualifications.

Whatever you do in your career as a project manager, make sure you work to find your own style. Learn from the project managers you've worked with in the past—think about what you want to emulate, and what you don't! If you can, find yourself a mentor—a more experienced project manager who can advise you on how to deal with tricky situations, or help you when you're not sure which tool will suit your needs best.

You needn't try to be an expert from the outset. Focus instead on improving with each project that you do, developing intuition about which tools to pick, how to handle tricky situations, and how best to achieve the project's ends.

But most of all, keep at it! Like any skill, project management takes practice to perfect. You should now have a solid foundation in the knowledge and skills required—from here, it will only get easier. Good luck!

# Appendix A: Tools

In this appendix, you'll find templates and examples for the key tools from each project phase. Where appropriate, there's also extra information and pointers to additional resources. This is intended as an easy reference guide to the tools—don't forget that if you need to understand more about why the tools are recommended, you'd do well to refer back to the original chapters where they were discussed.

# Initiating

Here's an outline of the tools that can help you during the project's initiation.

## Project Proposal Template

This template is designed to guide you as you prepare your project proposal.

### Proposed Project

In this section, briefly outline the project you're proposing. A couple of sentences describing what the project will be about should be sufficient. Think of it as the "elevator pitch" for your project—how you'd describe it if you only had two minutes to do so.

### Background

Give some background information that's primarily focused on the problem to be solved by the project. If the circumstances surrounding the project are particularly complex, you might choose to divide this section into a general description of the context, and an outline that details exactly what problem is to be solved.

### Value Creation

Since at this stage there will have been limited investigation into the value creation potential of the project, focus this section on providing an idea of what type of value the project has (for example, the potential cost savings and/or productivity improvements), and an order of magnitude estimate of that potential value. For instance, you might indicate that the project would save $1-200,000, or that the workload currently undertaken by two or three full-time employees, would be eliminated.

## Resources Required

In order to illustrate the possible return on investment, you also need to indicate what kinds of resources your project will need. This information will also help the organization to prioritize different projects it's considering. As an example, you might indicate that you need three people and a budget of approximately $50,000. Any specialist resources (be it equipment, consultants, or similar) that you expect will be required should be mentioned here as well.

# Measuring Value Creation

Broadly speaking, value comes in two flavors: hard and soft. **Hard value** indicates cash savings or additional income. **Soft value** usually indicates time or effort savings that won't necessarily translate immediately into cash.

As an example, a project might save $100,000 in direct costs (such as licenses, fees, production costs, or similar) and improve efficiencies. Efficiency improvements are often measured as a percentage of a job role—the assumption is made that you're saving "half a person," or something similar. Some organizations translate this value into actual savings as well (claiming the reduction in salary costs and so on), but many just redirect that existing effort to new endeavors, so the actual savings don't ever actually reach the bottom line.

There are a number of standard approaches to reflecting value. Below I've included a brief summary of what each one actually means, as well as a pointer to resources to teach you more if you need to. Typically, you'd want a financial analyst, or someone with similar skills, to perform the actual calculations, since they'll have the required expertise.

**net present value (NPV)**
>   NPV gives you the present value of the project, taking into account the income that's generated (or costs saved) over a number of years, less the costs of the project and any ongoing operational costs. An NPV that's greater than zero indicates that the project is viable; if the figure's less than zero, the benefit does not outweigh the costs of the project.

## internal rate of return (IRR)

IRR reflects the benefits of undertaking the project as a "rate of interest" on the money spent on the project. So, for instance, a project with an internal rate of return of only 2% might not be undertaken, because the money could be invested externally for a greater return. When comparing projects, the one with the higher IRR is usually the one to undertake.

## benefit cost ratio

As the name implies, this is a ratio that compares the benefits of the project against its costs. Projects with a benefit cost ratio that's greater than 1 are desirable.

## payback period

This figure reflects the length of time that it takes for the project to "earn back" its cost. So if your project is estimated to create an extra $10,000 of value per year, but the original cost was $50,000, the payback period will be five years.

## opportunity cost

This figure represents the cost of choosing one project (or opportunity) over another. This is why it is still important to choose the best option, not just the first viable project according to the financial metrics.

For further details of these metrics, including formal definitions and exact formulae, the best references tend to be finance and accounting texts. A primer I find useful is *Accounting for Non-Accounting Students, Fifth Edition*, by J.R. Dyson.[1] There are also plenty of books in the "finance for non-finance managers" genre as well.

---

[1] Harlow, Financial Times Prentice Hall, 2001

# Project Organization Chart

There's no set standard for a project organization chart—the main thing you need to consider is what will make sense for the people who are reading it. If you have a lot of people on the project, cramming them all into a graphical representation may not make sense. You might instead choose to produce a chart that shows the groups that are involved with the project, followed by a list of who's included in each group.

As a reminder, figure Figure A.1 is the project organization chart example that we saw in Chapter 2.

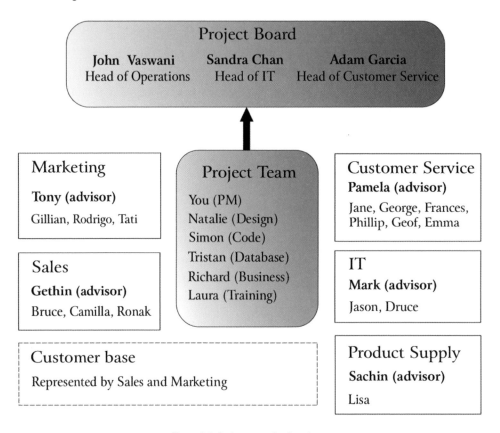

Figure A.1. Project organization chart

# Communication Plan Template

## Table A.1.

| Description | Frequency | Method | Audience | Owner |
|---|---|---|---|---|
| Name of the communication | How often it will happen | Method of communication | Who will receive the communication | Who is responsible |
| Project team meeting | Daily | Meeting | Project team | Project manager |
| Stakeholder update | Monthly | Email newsletter | Stakeholders | Project manager |
| Board meeting | Every two weeks | Meeting | Project board | Project manager |
| Contribution to department newsletter | Quarterly | Section of newsletter | Wider development | Project manager to deliver to department administration |

 ## Beware of the Biweekly Meeting

Be wary of using the term "biweekly" since it has dual meanings—it can mean "twice per week" and "every two weeks." For clarity, it's best to use an unambiguous term (such as "every two weeks"), or to spell out what you mean.

# Project Initiation Document

Here's an example of a Project Initiation Document.

## Example A.1. An Example Project Initiation Document

**Project Initiation Document**

*Customer Service Modernization Project*

**BUSINESS NEED (WHY)**

Currently, the customer service division performs a lot of manual work. Each person in the CS team spends more than a day a week dealing with paperwork, when the primary focus should be customer interaction. Tracking orders, queries, and complaints is difficult, and a lot of time is spent manually pulling together information so that reporting can be completed. When answering a call, the customer service agent isn't able to see all of the recent orders, queries, and complaints for the given customer, so customers often have to repeat information depending on who they speak to.

In addition, there's no linkage between the CS and inventory systems, so each day a number of calls have to be fielded by the product supply team just so that those taking orders can check that there are sufficient stocks to fulfill the order before placing it. Customers have also fed back via the sales teams and their customer service contacts that they would like to be able to place orders and log queries and complaints online or via email, rather than having to call the organization each time.

## PROJECT OBJECTIVE (WHAT)

*TO:* modernize the customer service processes and systems

*IN A WAY THAT:*

- removes manual rework from the processes and procedures

- effectively connects ordering, inventory, and customer query systems

- provides appropriate reporting and tracking of customer orders, queries, and complaints

- allows customers to interact via telephone, email, or web phone, both to make initial contact and to check for updates

*SO THAT:*

Customer satisfaction is increased to a score of 60% and running costs are decreased by $20 000 per annum.

## PROJECT DELIVERABLES (HOW)

- evaluation and recommendation as to whether to implement a generic CRM solution or whether to build one internally

- analysis of existing customer service processes and procedures and recommendation for improvements

- implementation of CRM solution in line with new processes and requirements

- interfaces to new CRM system from inventory and other existing systems

- customer-facing web site and email address for logging orders, queries, and complaints, as well as for status updates

## ESTIMATED TIMELINE (WHEN)

Since significant investigatory and analysis work needs to be done, there's a great deal of uncertainty in terms of how long this project will take. The recommendation is to set a deadline for the first two deliverables (identifying whether to buy or build a CRM solution and analyzing and recommending changes to the processes and procedures of the customer service department) of March 1st (two months from now). At this point, a plan for further work will be presented for Project Board review.

## PROJECT ORGANIZATION (WHO)

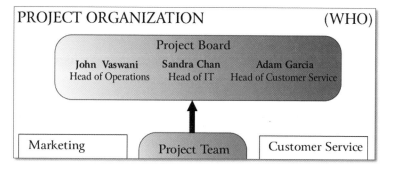

Figure A.2. Project organization chart (abbreviated)

## Typical Kickoff Meeting Agenda

Here's an agenda template for the project kickoff meeting.

**1. welcome and introduction**

> A good time to make sure that everyone understands who will be involved in the project

**2. project initiation review**

> Hand out copies of the project initiation document and review it with the team. This is important in making sure everyone is aligned on the purpose of the project.

**3. project approach**

> Explain how the project will be undertaken. Depending on your organization, you might want to start at the basics, explaining the phases the project will go through as well as the specifics of the project itself.

**4. communication plan**

> Explain when everyone who's present can expect to have future updates on the project's progress. Those who just want to be kept informed will then know exactly when and how this will happen.

**5. plan moving forward**

> Explain what the project team will be working on next. Identify whether or not any of the stakeholders' input will be needed in the immediate future.

# Planning, Executing, and Controlling

These tools and templates will help you through the project's Planning, Executing, and Controlling phases.

## Project Plan Template

It's possible to create a very long and involved project plan, but in the interests of the document remaining useful, it's usually best to keep the plan as short as possible. Include details of the tools that you'll use to keep track of deliverables, timings, and so on, either electronically if you're sharing the information online, or as appendices if the plan is printed out.

**deliverables and milestones**

Detail the top-level deliverables, highlighting any key milestones. In the interests of brevity, you may want to attach the full list, which you may choose to represent as a work breakdown structure.

**schedule**

Again, keep the level of detail appropriate. You probably want to show the main schedule phases and attach the full Gantt chart. As project phases are completed, you can add color-coding to reflect phases' status.

**assumptions and constraints**

This section need be no more than a bullet-point list of the key assumptions and constraints. Unless the project is particularly complex, you should aim to keep these lists short (a maximum of five to seven points).

**risk management plan**

Highlight the key risks and mitigations, and attach the full risk management plan. If there are only a few risks to mention, you could detail them in full.

# Work Breakdown Structure

Figure A.3 shows an example of a work breakdown structure.

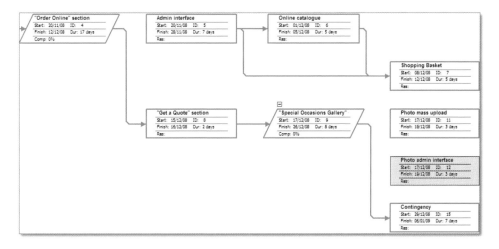

Figure A.3. Example work breakdown structure

# Gantt Chart

Figure A.4 shows an example of a Gantt chart.

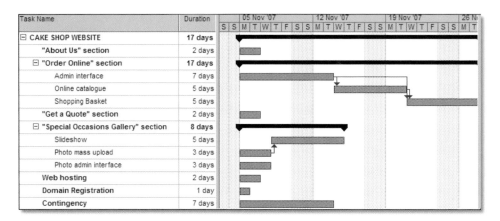

Figure A.4. Example Gantt chart

# Risk Management Plan Template

The project's risk management plan could contain these sections:

**risk list**

The complete list of risks that were identified, along with their respective "scores" (whether they're rated on a scale of "very low" to "very high," or a numbered scale). It makes sense to highlight those that were deemed to be above the "risk threshold" that was set for the project. You could use a grid to plot the risks and show which ones you've planned for.

**approach taken**

This section explains how the risks were identified, and how you identified which risks you would, and would not, plan for.

**contingency plans**

Provide contingency plans for those risks you decided to address. You may have decided to take some proactive action against the eventuality of some risks (for example, buying insurance)—document what you've done in these cases.

# Balance Quadrant

The balance quadrant depicted in Figure A.5 is explained in detail in Chapter 4.

Figure A.5. The balance quadrant

# Estimation Techniques

There are two different methods of estimation:

1. **Top-down estimation** involves the production of estimates at a project-phase level, rather than at an individual-deliverable level. This type of estimation should only be undertaken when you can base your estimates on similar past projects for which you have collected data.

2. **Bottom-up estimation**, the type of estimation we considered in Chapter 3, occurs when the person responsible for the work that will be done estimates how long it will take.

### Don't Double Count!

If you're using the bottom-up estimation approach, as you will for most projects, it's important to make sure that contingency isn't being added twice—sometimes, individuals will add contingency to their own tasks, and you'll add contingency periods to the whole schedule. Of course, this double-counting makes the timings bloated. On one hand, you'll have more time than you need, but on the other, your clients will start to get suspicious about all the padding, as you deliver faster than expected!

A number of different techniques are used for estimating. I've summarized the main categories below, but for more detailed information, many books deal solely with the question of estimation—*The Project Management Book of Knowledge* that the Project Management Institute provides, for example, is a good source of more detailed information.[2]

### expert judgment

Expert judgement is an analogous method in which the expert provides an estimate for a given task or deliverable based on their past experience of similar situations. If you have historical information from past projects, you can apply this to create an estimate as well (although an expert opinion of how analogous the tasks are is still needed).

### parametric estimation

This mathematical modeling technique takes the key project factors (such as cost per meter, or units per hour) into account. This approach tends to be easier to use in more conventional projects ("each worker can lay 60 bricks per hour") than knowledge work ("each programmer can write 60 lines of code per hour") because of the unpredictability of problem solving tasks.

### three-point estimates

A three-point estimate involves taking optimistic, most likely, and pessimistic estimates, and averaging them. As discussed in Chapter 3, a common way to create such an estimate is to weight the optimistic and pessimistic estimates by 1, and the most likely estimate by 4, dividing the total by 6.

It's important to remember that your chosen method of estimation should match the sophistication of your project! It's no good coming up with a parametric model to determine estimates if your team will neither understand nor respect them.

## Issue List Template

A table is usually the best representation for your issue list, as Figure A.6 indicates.

---

[2] Newton Square: Project Management Institute, 2004

| # | Description of Risk or Issue | Priority | Owner | Need Board Action? | Next Steps / Resolution | Start Date | Target Date | Resolved Date | Status |
|---|---|---|---|---|---|---|---|---|---|
| 1 | Content deadlines not being met | Med | Kate | No | Kate to pull together workshop to blitz through all the writing | 06-Nov-08 | 10-Nov-08 | | WIP |
| 2 | scrummycakes.com domain not available | High | Meri | Yes | Board selected justdelish.net from alternatives proposed | 02-Nov-08 | 15-Nov-08 | 11-Nov-08 | Closed |

Figure A.6. An example issue list showing the template in action

An typical issue list would contain the following columns:

## number

A unique issue number helps you to reference issues easily. As issues will not necessarily be resolved in the order in which they're listed, a unique issue ID also helps you to find open issues among those that are already closed.

## description

This area contains a concise description of the issue. If there's a need for an in-depth problem statement (which is unlikely except in very complex situations), you can attach this and include a simple description in the reference. The description should be sufficiently detailed that it allows team members to remember what the problem is when discussing issues in regular project meetings.

## priority

You can use any priority scale you choose (Low, Medium, High generally works fine), but you should set expectations of what the priority levels mean. It's easy for everyone who's logging an issue to think it's the most important problem, but having an issue list that consists only of high-priority issues makes it very difficult to prioritize the issues—especially a number of those listed have been assigned a false sense of urgency.

## owner

This field allows you to identify the person who's responsible for the next steps needed either to work out a solution to the issue, or implement a solution. Ideally, you want one owner for the course of the issue, but in some circumstances you might find that it works best if the issue's ownership changes once the solution has been worked out. For instance, you might need an expert to analyze the problem, but another member of the team may be able to implement a solution once it's been identified.

### need board action?

This column is primarily an indicator for you. This column allows you to identify the issues that need to be brought to the board's attention, either because the board members need to make a decision before you can move forward, or because they actually need to do something (such as allocating extra budget) in order for the project to continue. If you have a particularly urgent issue that needs board action, you might call an extraordinary board meeting, rather than waiting for the next one that's scheduled.

### next steps/resolution

This column contains details of what's being done next to investigate or resolve the issue. Once an issue is closed, you should also document the resolution, in case a similar situation occurs again, either in this project or a future one.

### start date

This area allows you to identify the date on which the issue was reported.

### target date

This area allows you to identify the date on which you intend to have resolved the issue.

### resolved date

This area allows you to identify the date on which the issue was actually resolved.

 **Date Patterns**

Having these three dates lets you see any patterns in your project. For instance, if issues are consistently being resolved the day after they are due, it probably means that they are not being worked on until right before the target date. This might be fine, but equally it might mean you need to discuss priorities with your team so that they give attention to high priority issues asap rather than just before the due date.

### status

This column reflects the current status of the issue. Since you have more detail in the next steps column, you can keep this one nice and simple, marking each issue either open (the issue has been recorded but nothing has been done yet),

WIP (the issue is a work in progress), or closed (either because the issue has been resolved, or because you have decided that it doesn't need to be addressed).

# Project Status Update Template

This template can be used to provide project stats updates.

**high-level status**

Use this section to summarize the current project status in one sentence. Accompany it with traffic-light color-coding to reflect that the project is on track (green), is experiencing some issues (yellow), or is off track (red).

**summary of achievements and issues**

This are comprises either a paragraph or some short bullet points that explain what has been achieved since the last project update, and detail the key issues that have been encountered.

**detailed status**

Typically, you'll want to show the overall status of the project here (perhaps including the high-level schedule with color-coding to show which phases are completed, and so on), and provide more details of the highest-priority issues.

**attachments**

You'll likely want to attach the most recent version of the project plan, issue list, and the Project Initiation Document for reference by recipients of your update.

# Change Request Template

The first part of the change request is filled in by the person who's proposing the change:

**proposer**

This space allows the identification of the person submitting the change for consideration.

**description**

This area facilitates a description of the change that's being requested. This description should be detailed enough for request to be understood and assessed.

**business benefit**

> This section allows for an explanation of the benefit this change will bring to the business, and/or the likely impact of not making the change.

**priority**

> The person who requests the change gives the request a priority, as seen from the business point of view. Typically, a scale of high, medium, and low ratings works fine.

The next two sections of the change request are filled out by the project team and project manager, based on how events play out following the request's submission:

**project team impact assessment**

> Once the project team members have considered the change, they write up a brief impact assessment. This assessment details the change's likely impact on the four areas of the balance quadrant—the project's scope, time, quality, and cost. The minimum investigation that's needed to give the board reasonable estimates upon which to base their decisions should be completed at this time. There's no sense spending a lot of time undertaking a detailed solution design, since the change may still be rejected at this point.

**board decision**

> Once the board have decided whether or not the change will be made, the decision and any supporting information is documented. This can be particularly helpful if a number of different stakeholders request very similar changes—you can share the outcome of the previous requests and potentially prevent others from wasting their time filling out new change requests.

# Planning Software

There's a multitude of options when it comes to planning software. The best place to start is to consider your own needs: how complex are the projects you will be managing? Do you expect to need to create multiple representations of each plan? How mature is your organization in terms of the project management techniques and tools it uses?

The second consideration is equally important: who will be reading the plan? The fastest way to render your plan obsolete is to make sure that you are the only person who can read it. The primary purpose of the project plan is to share information—if you choose a tool that's costly, or one with which your team, board, and stakeholders are unfamiliar, you'll either hinder the flow of information or stop it completely.

The best compromise is probably to pick a tool that meets your own needs when you're pulling together the Gantt chart, WBS, and other documents, but allows you to export those representations easily for sharing purposes. Some of the tools on the market will produce documents that can only be read by others with the same software—be aware of this when you are choosing your software tools.

Let's take a look at some of the most popular options for planning software, both on the desktop and online:

**Microsoft Project**

Microsoft Project, depicted in Figure A.7, is probably the most well-known piece of project software.[3] It's extensive and versatile, but over the years, it has grown to the point that it can now be very confusing for a new user. In deference to this situation, a guide has been developed that's now an integral part of the software, helping to step you through the process of making your plan.

There's also a significant license fee for this software—you'll need to factor that in, especially if you want to be able to share your documents for editing with the broader team. Project has some export features, but they're variable in terms of their usefulness. In particular, exporting a Gantt chart for editing in another piece of software is a challenge. The software is available for both Windows and Mac, although it seems that Merlin is very popular as a native Mac-based alternative.[4]

If all you really need is to put your plan into a Gantt chart, you could very easily go for a cheaper, simpler tool such as GanttProject. However, if you want to try out Microsoft Project, a 30-day trial is available from the Microsoft Project web site.

---

[3] http://office.microsoft.com/project/

[4] http://www.projectwizards.net/

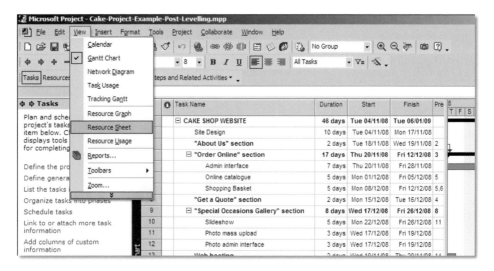

Figure A.7. The Gantt chart view in Microsoft Project, showing the other views available

### GanttProject

This free, open-source piece of planning software was developed in Java, so it offers the clear advantage that it can be run on Linux, Windows, or Mac. For diverse teams working on different platforms, this can be a big advantage.

Although it's not as fully-featured as Microsoft Project, GanttProject offers much more than just the basics, and should be more than adequate for anyone starting out managing small- to medium-sized projects.

My suggestion would be to try out a tool like GanttProject first, unless another piece of software is already in use for project work in your organization. The software is interoperable with Microsoft Project (you can import or export Project files easily), you can always take the work you've done so far with you if you need to move on to Project at some point. Since Microsoft Project was very much the original standard, most other planning software packages allow import or export, if not full interoperability.

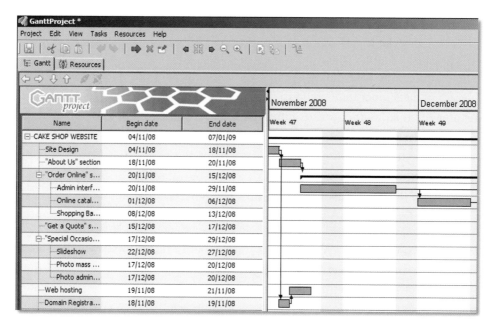

Figure A.8. The Gantt chart view in GanttProject

In addition to software programs like these, which operate on the desktop, online tools are available:

**Basecamp**

An online tool that's rapidly gaining popularity as a replacement for traditional project management software, Basecamp is best described as a blend of project management, personal productivity, and client portal software[5]. It's intended as a one stop shop for your project. It can be used by an unlimited number of people, as the pricing plans depend on the number of projects that you have active in your account. The free version of the software allows just one project to be run.

Basecamp is designed to act as the nexus for your project. Hence, it may be particularly useful for teams that want to use a shared online tool to focus their work—freelancers or those working remotely will find this option especially attractive. As always, the old caveat applies: you need to know your stakeholders

---

[5] http://www.basecamphq.com/

well enough to know whether they'll embrace this fully online solution, or will instead resist it and comment that Microsoft Project prints better!

There are of course a number of other tools that are not designed specifically as project management tools, but are flexible enough to be used for that purpose. The regular Microsoft Office suite of applications can serve quite well—Excel, or any other similar spreadsheeting tool, is useful for creating Gantt charts, unless you have a large number of dependencies that you want to account for automatically. Likewise, flowcharting tools like Visio[6] or Omnigraffle[7] can be used to create Work Breakdown Structures as well as organization charts. At a pinch, even Powerpoint will do for the latter!

Whatever you choose for your project, remember to think about who will be using it and how it will be used in the course of the project. The more complex the tool, the more options it provides users, so in some cases it may make sense to cut down the uncertainty for those working with the planning software you choose by providing guidelines.

## Tracking Software

Most project planning software also serves very well as project tracking software. As you move from the Planning phase into Executing and Controlling, simply adding ownership and status data to your existing schedules is the easiest way to keep track of the project.

Issue tracking and budget tracking are slightly different tasks. Most of the time, all you'll need is a simple spreadsheet, complemented by the issue list template we discussed above, and whatever calculations are needed for budget tracking.

At some point, however, things will become so complex that you'll want to consider other tools. If you have a very large project, involving lots of people who are spread around different locations discovering issues, you might choose to employ an online issue tracking tool of some description. There are a number of options, ranging from the proprietary and costly, through to the open source and free.

---

[6] http://office.microsoft.com/visio/
[7] http://www.omnigroup.com/applications/omnigraffle/

Similarly, you might choose to conduct your budget tracking in an accounting package rather than keeping track via a spreadsheet. I haven't come across any packages that are particularly useful for project budget management, but by the same token, things need to become fairly complex before you actually need specialist software!

As with the planning software packages we discussed, whatever tracking software you choose, the ability to share the documents between team members is paramount. Choose the software that makes it as easy as possible to achieve that aim over specialist features that you'll rarely use.

# Closing

These are the key tools that will help you through the closing phase of the project life cycle.

## Project Sign-off Template

The project sign-off template includes the following sections:

**project summary**

> This high-level summary details what the project was about, and what has been achieved. Your summary should touch on all four areas of the balance quadrant: scope, time, cost, and quality. Below the summary, there should be space where the board members can sign to document their official approval that the project has been completed.

**high-level deliverables**

> This section includes a list of the tasks, products, or items that have been delivered through the course of the project. Your aim here should be to document the scope that has been delivered, not relive the details of the project.

**original scope (Project Initiation Document)**

> Attach your original scope document, which (depending on the level of detail) may simply be your Project Initiation Document. This should closely mirror the list of deliverables outlined in the section above, as this reflects what was actually delivered.

**change log**

This section gives you the opportunity to list the changes that were accepted by the board, and affected the project's delivery. The intention is to document the original scope of the project and the subsequent changes made through the change process. The combination of the original scope information and the change log should result in the high-level deliverables you've listed.

# Customer Feedback Questionnaire Template

The first section of this document, shown in Figure A.9, is structured to gather quantitative feedback on various aspects of the project process. The example here is very generic, you might want to tailor your questionnaire further depending on your project and your stakeholder group's areas of specific focus and concern.

## STAKEHOLDER FEEDBACK FORM

NAME (Optional): _____     ORGANIZATION: _____

Please rate your level of agreement with the following statements by ticking the appropriate box

| Project Organization | Strongly Agree | Agree | Uncertain | Disagree | Strongly Disagree |
|---|---|---|---|---|---|
| I was clear on the point of the project | | | | | |
| I felt involved in the project from the start | | | | | |
| I was well-informed about project progress | | | | | |
| I understood the change management process | | | | | |
| Any changes I submitted were dealt with appropriately | | | | | |
| The project has delivered what it was meant to | | | | | |
| I agree that the project was closed at the appropriate time | | | | | |
| The project handover was complete and rigorous | | | | | |

Figure A.9. Quantitative part of the customer feedback questionnaire

The second half of the questionnaire, shown in Figure A.10, is more free-form, as it aims to encourage qualitative feedback.

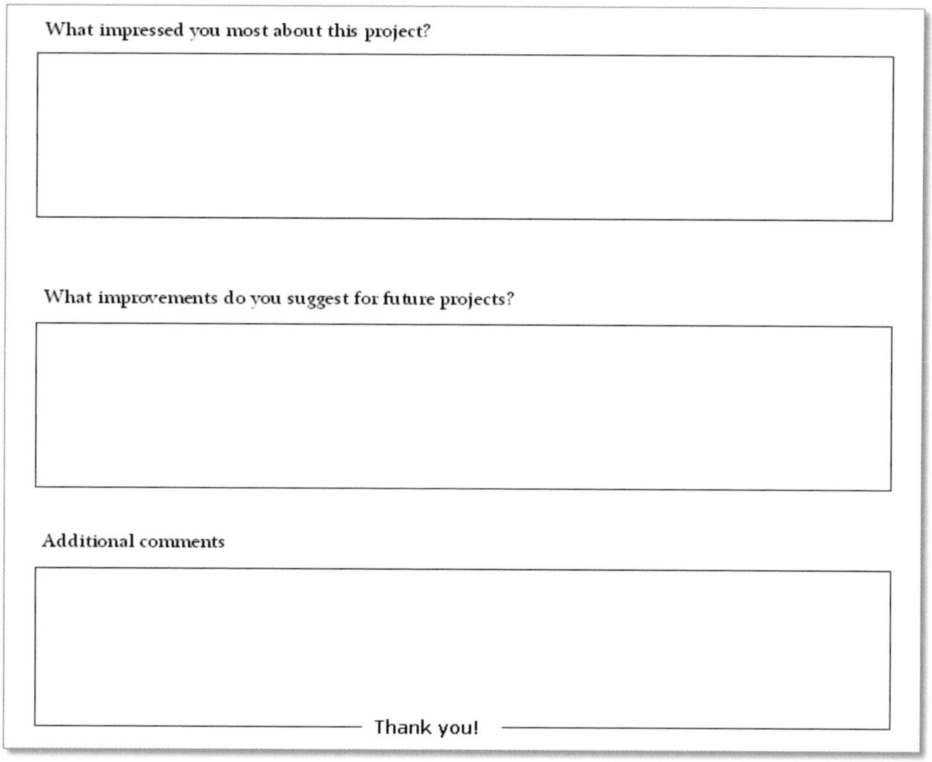

What impressed you most about this project?

What improvements do you suggest for future projects?

Additional comments

Thank you!

Figure A.10. Qualitative part of the feedback form

# Lessons Learned Summary Template

The basic format for the lessons learned summary is as follows:

**background**

Aim to describe the background of the project, and the project itself, in no more than a paragraph. The key is to give sufficient context for the lessons learned to make sense, without including extraneous detail.

**lessons learned**

Here, include a bullet-point list of what worked well, and what didn't. You might choose to group these points either as successes and mistakes, or by project stage. Focus on the actions or strategies that worked (or didn't) rather than the detail of who did what and when.

**recommendations**

Some of the lessons learned will suggest changes that could be made to the way that processes and systems in your project organization work. List any recommendations you're making here, but make sure to follow up by taking the best ideas and suggesting them to the appropriate person in your organization.

# Project Documentation Template

Your final project documentation should include this information:

**table of contents**

There will be a lot of content here, so make it easy for people to find what they're looking for.

**project documents**

Include every document that you've maintained during the project. At a minimum, you should include:

- Project Initiation Document

- project plan (with subsequent tracking from Executing and Controlling)

- change log

- issue list

- project updates

- project board meeting notes (these are the meetings in which key decisions were likely made; you may decide to include all your meeting notes, but this might be overkill)

- project sign-off

- lessons learned summary

**handover and training documents**

The exact nature of your project and your future role in the ongoing operations and support will dictate the kind of documentation and training that has been prepared. Whatever it is, include it all in the project documentation!

The most likely questions that will arise after you've moved on to a new project will be operational queries, which these documents should address. Other likely questions will focus on key decisions that were made in the course of the project (especially why certain scope items were included or excluded), which is why including the change log and issue list is so important.

# Appendix B: Resources

This appendix offers pointers to books, blogs, and web sites that you can access for more information on various topics we've touched on in this book. The project management resources range from refresher material, which is useful to consider when you're starting a new project, to pointers towards more advanced information. In very complex projects, you may find that you want some more rigorous "hard-core" tools at your disposal.

Also included here are resources relating to personal productivity and people management. One feature that's common to all the great project managers I've worked with is that they are personally very organized. Being able to keep on top of all the details is a good skill to develop, and the resources below will point you in the right direction.

Although people management is often not a direct responsibility of the project manager, many of these tools will be useful if you're managing the human component of your projects as well as the technical or work components. Developing these kind of soft skills can equip you with a better range of techniques for dealing with your project team, stakeholders, and board members.

## Books

**Gary R. Heerkens, *Project Management: 24 Steps to Help You Master Any Project* (New York: McGraw Hill Professional, 2007)**

> This great refresher text is short and to the point. It covers 24 mistakes that you could make in your project, and focuses on how to avoid them using positive practices. It's nice to read as a reminder of what's important when you're starting a project, or when you want to be convinced that cutting corners will only lead to pain.

**Ken Schwaber, *Agile Project Management with SCRUM* (Redmond: Microsoft Press, 2004)**

> SCRUM is one of the most promising agile software development methods around today. If you're doing technical work, it's definitely worth investigating. Even in non-technical projects, SCRUM offers much that's worth reapplying.

One of the challenges of agile methods, however, is that to use them, some adaptation of typical project management practices is needed. This book serves as an introduction to SCRUM development and teaches you all about managing projects without stifling their agility.

**Scott Berkun, *The Art of Project Management* (Sebastopol: O'Reilly, 2005)**

Focusing more on the soft skills and finesse that are the hallmarks of talented and experienced project managers, this book is a good one to read once you have some projects under your belt.

**Project Management Institute, *A Guide to the Project Management Book Of Knowledge (PMBOK Guide)* (Newton Square: Project Management Institute, 2004)**

The PMBOK is the official tome of the Project Management Institute. Detailed and comprehensive, it's best used as a reference unless you're using it as a cure for insomnia. If you start to feel that you need more rigid, hard-core tools, this is a good place to start. The overriding principle remains, though: don't adopt any approach or practice that isn't useful and maintainable.

**David Allen, *Getting Things Done: The Art of Stress-Free Productivity* (London: Piatkus Books, 2002)**

Getting Things Done (GTD) is a comprehensive system for personal productivity that has become very popular recently. The main tenet of the approach is that we suffer stress by trying to remember everything that we need to do. Capturing everything via project lists, to do lists, and reminder systems helps us to be better organized *and* less stressed. Having well-defined ways of handling your personal productivity can also help you to be a better project manager.

**Tom DeMarco and Timothy Lister, *Peopleware: Productive Projects & Teams* (New York: Dorset House Publishing, 1999)**

Peopleware was one of the first books aimed at the technical coders, engineers, and other normal workers making the transition from being "workers" to a "managers." Covering a wide variety of topics, including everything from how to make your people feel important to designing smart office spaces, it's a great primer for those who are new to management, and is written in a down-to-earth style with minimal management speak.[1]

---

[1] In fact, Tom DeMarco has written a number of excellent management books including *The Deadline* (a management novel) and *Slack*.

**Michael Lopp, *Managing Humans* (Berkeley: Apress, 2007)**
This book comprises a very readable collection of anecdotes from a software engineering manager. Along with a healthy dose of entertainment and humor, you also get a variety of tools and approaches for dealing with different people management scenarios.

# Blogs and Web Sites

**43Folders, at http://www.43folders.com/**
43Folders is a web site that's dedicated to the Getting Things Done approach, and is run by a disciple of the system, Merlin Mann. The site helps to provide a more in-depth understanding of the tools of GTD (as well as overviews for those who are new to the basic concepts), and lists helpful hints and tricks, as well as reviews of software that can help to support you.

**Lifehacker, at http://www.lifehacker.com/**
The only problem with the Lifehacker web site is that it offers almost too much information. The site is updated numerous times every day with tips, tricks, and techniques for "hacking your life," and making you more effective and efficient. It's useful to dip into now and again, or to use as a first place to start looking for a solution to a particular problem. You can also subscribe to authors or topics—in particular, editor Gina Trapani's longer pieces are especially good.

**Joel on Software, at http://www.joelonsoftware.com/**
Joel Spolsky runs his own software development business, and dispenses guru-like advice to his readership via his web site, Joel on Software. Full of great articles on everything from technical topics through to designing an office that will help you get the most out of your work force, it's well worth reading.

**Rands in Repose, at http://www.randsinrepose.com/**
Rands is the alter-ego of Michael Lopp, who wrote the *Managing Humans* book listed above. In fact, his web site, Rands in Repose, came first, and many of the biting anecdotes in the book started out on the site. This site is worth reading for its helpful advice, as well as the enduring sense that everything can be fixed. The good humor also improves your day!

**Chief Happiness Officer, at http://positivesharing.com/**

Alexander Kjerulf believes that being happy at work is important not only for an employee's wellbeing, but in order for the organization to deliver the best results. I'm inclined to agree with him even if occasionally his positive attitude almost becomes too much! There's still enough good content here for the site to be worthy of regular visits.

**Slacker Manager, at http://www.slackermanager.com/**

Taking a much more cynical tone than the Chief Happiness Officer, Slacker Manager is still ripe with advice and pointers to other books or blogs. The subjects covered are broad-ranging, covering everything from personal productivity and careers, to people management and employee engagement. Start with the "best of" category.

**Geek | Manager, at http://blog.geekmanager.co.uk/**

This is my own site, where I mainly talk about my own experiences and the steep learning curve I've traversed from starting out as a computer geek, to becoming a project and people manager.

**Linked In, at http://www.linkedin.com/**

Linked In is a social networking site for your work life. For those who are just starting out as project managers, it can be very helpful for finding others who can help you with advice. Even if you don't know any experienced project managers, chances are that someone you know does. Linked In can help you make connections with friends of friends or colleagues, whose experiences can help you. You might even find that there are enough young project managers in your area to warrant meeting up to swap war stories over a beer every now and again.

# Appendix C: Professional Qualifications

There are a couple of prominent professional project management bodies and associations. As you develop as a project manager, you may want to invest in a professional qualification—especially if project management is becoming the main focus of your career.

The relative importance of professional qualifications will depend on a number of things: your location, industry, level of experience, and so on. The best advice is to try and understand the value of the qualification or certification before you invest time in obtaining it. Some industries require project managers to hold professional qualifications—a fact that's often reflected in job descriptions—whereas others are more interested in the actual experience you have. Ask around to work out what will be the best approach for your personal circumstances.

## Associations and Qualifications

PMI, the **Project Management Institute**[1] is probably the most well-known of the international professional associations. The majority of its membership is in North America, although there are significant numbers of members in both Asia Pacific and EMEA (Europe, the Middle East, and Africa). There are hundreds of local chapters, an d many special interest groups that focus on a particular topic, be it a specific industry, diversity concern, or other hot issue.

PMI provides both the Project Management Professional (PMP) and Certified Associate in Project Management (CAPM) qualifications. The PMP qualification is one of the most widely recognized internationally, and guarantees a level of experience as well as knowledge, since in order to sit the PMP exam you have to have documented a certain number of hours of project management experience.

Typically, in order to attain the required level of experience, you'll need to have worked as a project manager for three to five years. The CAPM qualification requires far less experience, so it's often used as an intermediary qualification by those who aren't yet experienced enough to sit the PMP.

---

[1] http://www.pmi.org/

The **International Project Management Association (IPMA)** is the oldest of the organizations, providing a framework for numerous local organizations worldwide.

The IPMA provides for four different levels of project management certification:

- IPMA-D, denoting a Certified Project Management Associate
- IPMA-C, for a Certified Project Manager
- IPMA-B, for a Certified Senior Project Manager
- IPMA-A, denoting a Certified Projects Director

Each certification level says something about the individual's amount of experience, as well as the degree of responsibility he or she holds. More information can be found on the association's web site.[2]

The **Association for Project Management**,[3] APM, is based in the UK and draws most of its membership from Europe. For those who are unlikely to work outside of this region, the strong network that APM provides may be desirable.

APM provides a series of qualifications in line with the IPMA four-level certification model, including APMP (IPMA-D), Practitioner Qualification (IPMA-C), and Certificated Project Manager (IPMA-B).

The **International Association of Project and Program Management (IAPPM)** was founded more recently (in 2003) and, as the name suggests, it focuses not just on individual project management, but also on broader program management. IAPPM provides the Certified Project Manager (CPM) certification.

---

[2] http://www.ipma.ch/
[3] http://www.apm.org.uk

# Glossary

assumptions
    beliefs about what is true, usually describing the context of a project; if assumptions turn out to be false, this can have significant impact on the project

balance quadrant
    a tool used to weigh up the impact of project decisions and changes on the time, cost, scope, and quality of the project

budget
    the total amount of resource dedicated to a project; often used simply to describe the cash available to pay for the project

bugs
    software imperfections

change request
    description of a change in project requirements, which, if approved, usually affects the project scope or quality in some way and may affect the cost and time dimensions of a project

closing
    the project phase in which the final activities are performed and the project is officially signed off

collaboration
    working with others to achieve a common goal

communication
    arriving at a shared understanding of a situation

communication plan
    a plan that describes how project communication will take place, listing the relevant meetings, emails, updates, and so on

constraints
    limitations that affect the project in some way; they are usually part of the context of a project and relate to either time, scope, cost, or quality

contingency
    the time allocated to unforeseen events and delays in the project schedule; the amount of time by which

| | |
|---|---|
| | deliverables can be delayed before the overall project schedule will be affected |
| controlling | project phase focused on keeping control of the project, where the key question to answer is "is the project on track?" |
| critical path schedule (CPS) | the longest chain of deliverables in the project; these deliverables result in an overall delay to the project if they slip |
| deliverables | the end products that make up your project |
| dependencies | cases in which work on one task or deliverable can't be started or completed before another task or deliverable has been completed |
| discovery | the process of finding potential projects to undertake |
| estimate | an approximate calculation of the time or budget needed to achieve a particular task or deliverable |
| executing | the project phase in which the plans are carried out and the majority of the actual work of the project is achieved |
| Gantt chart | a bar chart representation of the project schedule |
| handover | the process by which a project is documented and responsibility is transferred to the ongoing operational or support team |
| initiating | the project phase in which the project is officially started |
| issue list | a list of the project issues that have been encountered, whether open, still works in progress, or already closed |

| | |
|---|---|
| issues | risks that have been realized during the course of the project |
| kickoff meeting | an initial meeting to kick-start the project, bringing together key project stakeholders |
| milestones | key dates, usually when a particularly important deliverable must be delivered |
| offshoring | business practice of moving work to another (typically lower cost) country |
| operational contract | contract that's put into place after the project has been completed, covering the ongoing day-to-day work |
| outsourcing | business practice of moving work to another company, typically in search of cost reductions |
| planning | the project phase concerned with breaking the project into manageable chunks and planning how best to proceed |
| portfolio planning | the process of planning an overall group of projects to be undertaken by an organization |
| project | a one-time effort to change the state of the world in some way; typically, projects either focus on producing something (a product) or on changing the way something is done (a process) |
| project board | the group of senior stakeholders (ideally just three) that will make key project decisions |
| project initiation document (PID) | a document summarizing the what, when, how, who, and why of the project |
| project life cycle | the phases that any project progresses through (Initiating, Planning, Executing, Controlling, and Closing) |

| | |
|---|---|
| project management | everything you need to make a project happen on time and within budget to deliver the needed scope and quality |
| project organization chart | a diagram showing everyone involved in the project, including the project team, project board, key stakeholders, and resources |
| project portfolio | a set of projects that are connected in some way, whether they're owned by the same organization or related in terms of the business benefits they will deliver |
| project sign-off | official confirmation that the project has been completed successfully, signed by the project sponsor |
| project sponsor | the senior supporter of the project, responsible for ensuring that there are sufficient resources and championing the business value the project will deliver to the organization |
| project team | the team responsible for delivering the project itself; may consist of people from different organizations or companies |
| project/business value | the reason for doing the project; the benefits that completing the project will bring to the organization |
| quality | the degree of excellence inherent in the project's product and process (can cover both the project approach and the deliverables themselves) |
| resource leveling | the process of reassigning work so that overloaded resources have a more normal or manageable workload |
| resources | the people, technology, space, tools and so on needed to complete project tasks and deliverables; |

|  | a generic term for anything used up by executing the project |
| --- | --- |
| risk | the possibility of the occurrence of an event that will have a negative effect on the project |
| rolling wave | a planning approach in which only the near future is planned in detail; work further out is only planned at a high level, with detailed planning being completed as the work's start date approaches |
| schedule | the part of the project plan that indicates the timings on which tasks or deliverables will be completed |
| scope | the description of the work that is and isn't included in the project; for a product this might be list of requirements or functionality that will be delivered; for a process, it will describe the areas that are and are not included |
| service level agreement (SLA) | agreement between the organizations providing and receiving support of what support will be provided and how quickly; for instance, it might specify that critical business issues will be resolved within 24 hours |
| stakeholders | all those interested in, affected by, or otherwise involved in the project |
| strategic | important to the future of an organization or person in some way |
| success criteria | the list of conditions that must be met for a project or endeavor to be deemed successful. For projects, these should be documented at the start of the project for clarity |
| tasks | the activities undertaken to achieve deliverables |

| | |
|---|---|
| validation | the process of checking that the project has met the underlying business need that it was intended to |
| value creation | the expression of the business benefit of the project, either in terms of cost savings, efficiency gains, increased sales, or reduced risk |
| verification | the process of checking that the project has delivered the scope that was promised; differs from validation in that it focuses on what was promised and what was delivered, rather than the underlying business problem to be solved |
| work breakdown structure (WBS) | expression of project scope broken down into a hierarchy of smaller deliverables |

# Index